YOUR KITCHEN GARDEN
Month-by-Month

Andi Clevely

YOUR KITCHEN GARDEN
Month-by-Month

Andi Clevely

David and Charles

'I have always thought a kitchen garden a more pleasant sight than the finest orangery.' JOSEPH ADDISON

A DAVID & CHARLES BOOK
© F&W Media International LTD 2010

David & Charles is an imprint of F&W Media International, LTD
Brunel House, Forde Close, Newton Abbot, TQ12 4PU, UK

First published in the UK in 2010
Reprinted in 2011

The text and images contained in this edition were first published as
The Kitchen Garden Month-by-Month

A catalogue record for this book is available from the British Library.

ISBN-13: 978-0-7153-3767-7 paperback
ISBN-10: 0-7153-3767-X paperback

Printed in China RR Donnelley for:
F&W Media International, LTD
Brunel House, Forde Close, Newton Abbot, TQ12 4PU, UK

Publisher: Stephen Bateman
Commissioning Editor: Freya Dangerfield
Art Editor: Martin Smith
Design: Diana Knapp
Artwork: Avis Murray
Editor: Verity Muir
Production Controller: Bev Richardson

Vegetable planting plan p120, courtesy of Janet Macdonald

F+W Media publishes high quality books on a wide range of subjects
For more great book ideas visit: www.rubooks.co.uk

CONTENTS

INTRODUCTION

SEASONS AND MONTHS

Every year is different in the kitchen garden. Spring can be late or autumn early, winter mild or the summer short. Under average conditions, however, the terms 'early', 'mid' and 'late' are used in this book to correspond approximately to the following months:

SPRING
Early: March
Mid: April
Late: May

SUMMER
Early: June
Mid: July
Late: August

AUTUMN
Early: September
Mid: October
Late: November

WINTER
Early: December
Mid: January
Late: February

SEED VARIETIES
Advice on choosing seeds is given elsewhere (see, for example, p44). The wide range available can be so bewildering, however, that several organisations have tested and selected outstanding varieties for general home use. These are often highlighted in seed lists and you can usually choose them with confidence – in the UK, for example, choice varieties may be identified by the initials RHS (Royal Horticultural Society) or NIAB (National Institute of Agricultural Botany), indicating their recommendation. Seedsmen themselves may also select varieties for special purposes or qualities: some might be more suitable for freezing or have very good flavour, while others noted for pest or disease resistance are ideal for organic gardeners. Many of these appear in the selections listed later in the book.

Growing your own food is compulsive. Despite being responsible for a large country estate, where everything from laying boundary hedges and pollarding riverside willows to deadheading rhododendrons and sowing summer bedding needs to be done at some time or other, my heart is in the kitchen garden. You will find me there first thing in the morning, quietly checking all is well. And at dusk as we make our way back to the tool shed, it is there among the vegetables, fruit and herbs that I am tempted to linger until it is too dark to see.

There are many reasons for this irresistible appeal of kitchen gardening. It has something to do with the creative need to work the soil with your own hands, care for the plants yourself, and finally gather in produce fresher than any you can buy. Perhaps there is even a little of the pioneering spirit that drives people everywhere to tame a patch of wilderness, and substitute disciplined rows of crop plants as evidence that it is still possible to produce at least part of one's basic necessities.

Whatever the motivation, it is hard to exaggerate the difference between tired shop produce and fresh home-grown lettuces that burst with flavour, young beans and juicy carrots so crisp that they snap almost at a touch, ripe fragrant melons still warm from the afternoon sun, and herbs that perfume the air and your hands with their lingering aromatic oils. Quality is what the kitchen garden is all about, and it is not difficult to achieve.

Anyone can grow their own vegetables, fruit and herbs. Given sprawling country acres and the whole day at your disposal, it is possible to be self-sufficient in food crops. If you have just a small backyard plot, a window box or a collection of pots, you can still grow a few herbs, summer salads and perhaps strawberries on a window-sill for a little self-indulgence. But whether the plants are integrated into existing flower beds and borders, or grown in a specially designated kitchen garden, most of us have enough room to grow at least a few favourite crops for a succession of produce all the year round.

Organising their cultivation is the subject of this book. Perhaps more than in any other field of gardening, timing is crucial for success with edible plants. Knowing when to prepare the ground and how early a crop can be sown, how long it will be before you can expect to start picking and when a follow-on sowing should be made, are all part of planning a steady continuity of produce from garden to kitchen. Avoiding embarrassing gluts and shortages is an imprecise art; weather, pests, diseases, and your own reserves of time and energy all influence timing. But there is more information accessible to gardeners than ever before to help with planning supplies month-by-month, and I have drawn on this extensively in the following pages.

Crop varieties available today are the result of generations of careful selection and breeding. Many of them were developed for commercial use, emphasising particular qualities such as reliable germination, uniform growth and pest or disease resistance. Some techniques – using cloches, horticultural fleece or biological pest control, for example – have also filtered through to gardeners from professional growers, and these are all worth using where appropriate as aids to success.

It is important though to balance the latest ideas with traditional skills and methods that are still valid or being rediscovered. Widespread interest in 'organic' gardening, for example, has revived the time-honoured belief in creating a fertile soil rather than simply feeding plants, and in controlling pests and diseases by methods that do not damage the environment. Concern for our own positive health has led to a reassessment of our diet, with a new emphasis on fresh vegetables and fruit grown with minimal use of chemicals.

Similarly, the frequently remarkable virtues of modern seed strains should not blind us to older kinds, sometimes known as 'heritage varieties', which possess qualities of their own. Uniformity and predictability are not everything: traditional varieties are sometimes variable in vigour and appearance, but they may be more reliably hardy or drought tolerant, or perhaps have more flavour, a quality often overlooked when breeding new strains. Above all, they are part of our heritage and help maintain the diversity that ensures we do not end up growing the same few varieties, all vulnerable to similar problems. Whenever possible I have included in the book both up-to-date and classic varieties that are suitable for home cultivation, together with traditional and modern techniques where relevant.

A kitchen garden is not just a place for growing vegetables. Apart from their other many uses, herbs are important culinary ingredients and gardeners usually grow at least a basic selection of these for gathering fresh and also for preservation by drying or some other method. Mint and parsley are included in the crop profiles because of their popularity, while others appear where appropriate in the Tasks of the Month sections. One of the projects is also devoted to introducing herbs to the kitchen garden, but so wide and varied is their range that you will need to consult a specialist handbook for full details (see Further Reading, p142).

The same advice applies even more to fruit crops. All the various kinds of fruit were traditionally grown in the kitchen garden, usually in ornamental forms such as espaliers and fans on walls and beside paths. Caring for them used to involve a lot of complex and skilled pruning and training to keep their growth under control, but modern dwarfing rootstocks have simplified their management to the point where gardeners are rediscovering the pleasure of growing choice varieties seldom available elsewhere. Strawberries, melons and rhubarb feature as crops, while fruit in general is discussed as a project.

Fruit is as stimulating to grow as any other crop, and eventually you might want to explore golden raspberries, greengages, white currants and other delicacies. One of the special joys of kitchen gardening is being able to choose what to grow – a favourite vegetable, an elusive herb cultivar or an unusual kind of fruit – and then to grow it in the best possible way. Most of us are fortunate enough to grow crops from choice rather than from necessity, and the enjoyment we get from this is an important motivation. The kitchen garden can be as attractive to look at as any flower bed or shrubbery, but the joy of tending and harvesting its crops is both a unique bonus and a perennial pleasure.

LOCAL VARIATIONS
Wide differences in temperature occur within a region, sometimes between adjacent gardens, and you should always adjust recommended sowing, planting and harvesting times, even the choice of crop or variety, to take account of local conditions such as the likelihood of frost in late spring and early autumn, prolonged winter freezing or summer droughts. Altitude is also an influence, every 300m (1,000ft) in height decreasing average temperatures by about one degree centigrade, while soils may differ in their suitability for particular varieties.

JANUARY

Mid-winter is a tough time for plants and gardeners alike. With growth at its lowest ebb, any stirrings of life are usually far out of sight underground. But even though the kitchen garden might appear bleak and uninviting, mid-winter weather has a benign influence on the soil and on the annual life cycles of plants. Low temperatures trigger positive responses in crops as varied as Brussels sprouts, garlic and apples, all of which are better for exposure to the cold. Frost thins pest populations and reduces sticky clay to a crumbly, more manageable texture, while winter rains top up the natural soil reservoir ready for the new season.

The weather this month also dictates how much you can do outdoors. There are often fine spells when the soil is dry enough to start cultivation for spring sowing and planting. A mild sunny day is ideal for seasonal fruit pruning, or simply getting the feel of the garden and visualising the crops you would like to grow and where to put them. It is advisable to plan well ahead in a kitchen garden, and should a sullen wind or shower of hail drive you indoors, there is plenty to do there in warmth and comfort. The Romans called this season Preparing Time, and while the bustle of spring is still weeks away you have the leisure to make plans for the approaching season, consider options and choose varieties, read widely about other people's methods and experiences, and above all order the seeds and plants that will transform your ideas into reality.

Even seasoned gardeners who have been feeding the family for many years sense the annual adventure that lies ahead. If you are new to kitchen gardening the challenge is greater still, but so are the rewards, for every fresh lettuce, sweetcorn cob or handful of runner beans you carry to the kitchen is a trophy that makes all this month's planning and preparation worthwhile.

APRIL

Enchanting but capricious is the best description of mid-spring. Some days you can step outside and sense that summer is only just round the corner, and everywhere plants will be bursting into life, with fruit trees and bushes in bloom, vegetable seedlings emerging while your back is turned, and herbs covered with soft young growth. Yet at other times the rhythm of the new season can stumble as sharp frost puts growth on hold and scorches tender young foliage, or heavy showers and chill winds send you scurrying for cover.

Under the influence of increasing temperatures and day length, soils become more receptive as the month progresses and there will be opportunities to catch up on sowings and plantings postponed from last month or even earlier. Mid-spring is a steady, exciting bustle: successional batches of crops such as carrots, peas and salads need sowing to maintain supplies later, and already it is time to start the last batch of broad beans. In mild areas runner beans may be sown later this month, a real hint of summer – looking even further ahead, maincrop potatoes and carrots for store are started now, together with all the various brassicas needed for winter use.

Despite the urgency to keep up the momentum, however, this is also a month to be enjoyed. One of the greatest pleasures now is scouring the garden for young spring produce to relieve the long season of winter vegetables. Carrots, lettuces and spring cabbages should be available, as well as outdoor rhubarb and perhaps a taste of forced strawberries under glass; towards the end of the month the first asparagus will be ready for cutting. In a good season there might even be a glut of one or two vegetables, for example, sprouting broccoli ready for cutting every other day, or radishes under glass maturing almost while you watch. With careful planning there need be no 'hungry gap' between winter crops and the new season's produce.

July

August

tasks
FOR THE
month
1

SOW

Aubergines, basil, beetroot, broad beans, Brussels sprouts, calabrese, carrots, cauliflowers, celeriac, celery, claytonia, coriander, corn salad, endive, French beans, good king henry, kale, kohlrabi, landcress, leaf beet, leeks, lettuces, mint, parsley, parsnips, peas, peppers, pickling onions, radishes, salsify, scorzonera, spinach, spring onions, sprouting broccoli, summer cabbages, swedes, tomatoes, turnips, winter cabbages.

PLANT

Asparagus, broad beans, bulbing onions, calabrese, carrots, endive, globe artichokes, kohlrabi, lavender, leaf beet, lettuces, maincrop potatoes, mint, summer cabbages.

HARVEST FRESH

Asparagus, broad beans, Brussels sprouts, carrots, cauliflowers, corn salad, good king henry, kale, landcress, leaf beet, leeks, lettuce, parsley, radishes, rhubarb, salad leaves, seakale, spinach, spring cabbages, spring onions, sprouting broccoli, turnip tops, turnips.

CHECKLIST

- Sow maincrop carrots for storing
- Protect early potatoes from frost
- Watch out for soil pests attacking seedlings
- Dig and prepare a trench for hardy celery
- Sow red cabbage for autumn and winter use
- Start spraying fruit against pests and diseases
- Thin seedlings in rows sown last month (see p45)
- Erect a protective screen around carrot seedlings (see p59)
- Start hoeing regularly to deter weeds (see p80)
- Pollinate strawberries growing in pots (see p11)
- Give frames and greenhouses a light shading

SOWING MAINCROP CARROTS

By sowing small batches of an early short variety every few weeks, you can maintain a continuous supply of sweet juicy 'bunching' carrots for much of the growing season, and even well into autumn from sowings in coldframes or under cloches. For storing in the ground or in boxes indoors, you need to grow a maincrop variety. Sometimes known as intermediate or long carrots, these take all season to produce the large heavy roots used in winter stews and casseroles. Sow this month (see p58), in a sheltered bed if roots are to be left in the ground over winter. Thin seedlings to about 4cm (1½in) apart initially, and after 10–12 weeks pull alternate roots for immediate use, leaving the rest to continue growing to full size.

PROTECTING POTATOES

Some gardeners finish planting early potatoes by mounding soil in a ridge along each row, and this is sometimes enough to keep the tubers in darkness, especially if sets are planted deeply. The young shoots above ground, however, are very sensitive to frost and when this threatens the best insurance is to earth them up and cover the stems. First hoe or lightly fork between rows to loosen the ground and disturb any weeds, and then use a draw hoe to pull soil almost to the top of the stems. In very severe conditions cover the tops completely with soil or a layer of dry straw, but expose the tips once more when the weather improves.

COUNTERING SOIL-BORNE PROBLEMS

As the ground warms up, so soil pests and diseases become active once more. A few simple precautions taken in time, however, can reduce any problems. Cultivate the soil regularly between rows to expose grubs and eggs for foraging birds, and when digging or preparing seedbeds watch out for larger pests such as vine weevils and leather-jackets. If you suspect the presence of pests (wire-worms, for example, after digging grassy ground), use a proprietary seed-dressing when sowing. Check the acidity of the soil regularly (see p32) to avoid nutrient deficiencies and brassica clubroot, and sprinkle lime over sowings of peas and beans as a slug deterrent. Clear exhausted crops and dead leaves that might shelter pests, and control weeds as these are often alternative hosts. Finally choose resistant crop varieties if problems such as root aphids and parsnip canker are prevalent.

DIGGING CELERY TRENCHES

Although plants will not be set out until after the last frosts, it is worth preparing a celery trench this month to

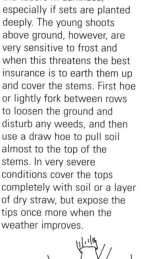

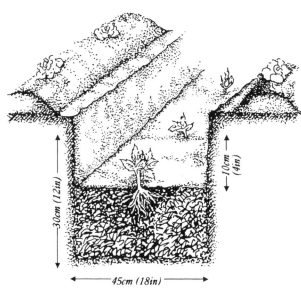

Celery trench with lettuces growing along the top

30cm (12in) · 10cm (4in) · 45cm (18in)

allow time for the soil to settle, and also to fit in a salad catch crop before earthing up starts.

■ Dig a straight trench about 45cm (18in) wide and 30cm (12in) deep, and work plenty of manure or compost into the bottom.

■ Backfill until the surface in the trench is about 10cm (4in) below ground level, and neatly mound the remaining soil in a ridge on both sides of the trench for earthing up plants later.

■ Lightly fork a little general fertiliser into these ridges, and then sow or transplant lettuces along the top – these will mature before the celery needs earthing up in the summer.

GROWING RED CABBAGE

Red cabbages are as easy to grow as their more common green relatives, and with their high vitamin C content are useful vegetables for autumn and winter use. All varieties can be sown now in the same way as for ordinary winter cabbages (see p126), either in a nursery bed outdoors or in modules in a coldframe. Transplant to prepared ground in late spring or early summer and keep well watered to make large heads for cutting from autumn onwards. Crops can be cleared in late autumn for storing in boxes of straw, and if kept cool and dry will last in good condition there until early spring. You can sow more in early autumn in a coldframe, planting these out early the following spring for summer use.

SPRAYING FRUIT

When you grow fruit it is important to decide if you are going to depend on natural predators and efficient management to avoid pest and disease problems (see p48), or to follow a chemical spray plan. There are certain critical times for spraying to best advantage.

Apples and pears – use a combined insecticide/fungicide against scab, mildew, aphids and other pests, spraying while flower buds are still in green clusters and again when buds first show colour.

Plums and cherries – spray with insecticide against aphids and caterpillars when green buds first appear.

Strawberries – spray now to treat aphids.

Raspberries – prevent fungal disease by spraying this month with a copper fungicide.

Gooseberries – use a fungicide to treat mildew before flowers open and again when the berries are visible.

Blackcurrants – spray with insecticide against big bud mite, first when flower buds are like tiny bunches of grapes and again a month later.

STRIP CROPPING WITH CLOCHES

To save time, plan crops so that cloches need only be moved from one set of plants to an adjacent row, rather than having to carry them round the garden. As an example, sow carrots and lettuce in late winter and cover until mid-spring, when sweetcorn is sown a short distance away and covered with the cloches. In early summer plant melons or peppers, and cover with cloches until cleared in early autumn, when the cloches can be transferred to late summer-sown carrots, radishes and spring onions; keep these cloched until used.

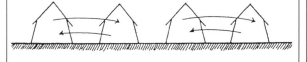

MULTIPLE SOWINGS
Some vegetables can be started as groups of seed sown in modules in a warm greenhouse, for planting out unthinned twice the normal distance apart to allow room for all the seedlings to develop. This economises on space, both in the greenhouse and outdoors, and allows an early start. Harden off and plant out under cloches if necessary to ensure unchecked growth. Suitable vegetables include beetroot, leeks, onions (maincrop and spring varieties), turnips and carrots (round varieties only).

BASIL, KING OF HERBS
A sun-loving herb from the Mediterranean, basil needs a long, warm growing season and is best started now. Sow small pinches of seed in small pots indoors in heat. Do not overwater seeds or seedlings or they will quickly rot. Pinch out tips of shoots when they have two pairs of true leaves to encourage branching, and also nip off any flower buds that appear later in the season. Keep growing in a sunny position and always water at midday, making sure you do not wet the leaves.

LOOKING AHEAD TO LATE SPRING

■ Make sure you have a supply of straw or special mats to protect strawberries as they ripen

■ If bad weather delays planting out, feed plants waiting in trays to keep them healthy

■ Inspect hosepipes and other watering equipment in case an early drought occurs

■ Check you have sown all the brassicas you need, as next month is the last chance if plants are to make a good size before winter

plants
OF THE
month
1

**MAIN CROP ROTATION
GROUPS (see p15)**

1 Legumes, onions
2 Brassicas
3 Root crops

ASPARAGUS
(Asparagus officinalis)

Once regarded as a luxury, this delicious vegetable does not need to be cultivated in traditional large beds. The decorative plants can be grown in groups or single rows, in a flower border if preferred, and will crop for 20–30 years. Spears are sometimes blanched (see p136).

type Hardy herbaceous perennial fern, producing edible young shoots or 'spears' from mid-spring until mid-summer

sowing and planting Plants are raised from seed or bought as 1- or 2-year-old crowns. Soak the large seeds in water for 48 hours, and then sow in a nursery bed in late spring, 2.5m (1in) deep and 8cm (3in) apart. Ordinary varieties stay there until the following spring; quality is variable, so only retain the strongest seedlings. Hybrids can be sown in late winter, in small pots under glass at 15°C (60°F), and if hardened off for planting out in early summer will crop lightly the following year.

Seedlings raised outdoors and bought crowns are planted in spring in holes deep enough for you to cover the tops of plants with about 15cm (6in) of soil. Plant crowns on a small mound with their roots spread out evenly and pointing slightly downwards. Space plants 45cm (18in) apart, in single or double rows or in small groups. Cover crowns after planting with a little soil, and add more as first stems grow until the ground is level once more

site Open sunny positions exposed to frost in winter but sheltered from cold winds in spring. All soils are suitable if well drained. Dig deeply well before planting, adding plenty of compost or manure, and lime acid soils to neutral readings

care Water and handweed the young plants until established. When the delicate foliage turns yellow in autumn, cut to ground level, weed thoroughly around plants and then mulch with decayed manure – alternatively feed with a general fertiliser in early spring and again after harvesting ends

harvest Cut spears with a knife about 5cm (2in) below soil level when they are 15–20cm (6–8in) tall. Cutting

continues for about eight weeks, up to the longest day when plants are then left to build up strength for the next season. One or two spears may be cut from strong hybrids the first year after planting; other kinds should be left to develop for a further season. You can gather more spears the following year over a 6-week season, with a full crop the year after

storage Asparagus may be frozen, especially if puréed for soup

pests and diseases The main problem is asparagus beetle, whose dark grubs feed on the fern and hibernate over winter in the soil; spray beetles and grubs with derris or pyrethrum

varieties Traditional kinds: 'Connover's Colossal', 'Martha Washington'. All-male hybrids: 'Accell', 'Boonlim', 'Cito', 'Dariana', 'Franklim', 'Lucullus'

comments Modern hybrids are all-male plants, and yield heavier crops at an earlier stage, whereas older kinds produce both male and female plants, the latter flowering and bearing red berries: these fruiting ferns and volunteer seedlings are best removed to prevent inferior plants from taking over. A little of the bright green ornamental fern may be cut for vases, but take care not to exhaust cropping plants

LETTUCE
(Lactuca sativa)

One of the most popular garden crops, it is available all the year round with careful planning. The bewildering choice and diversity of varieties can be simplified into a few basic categories. Heading or hearted kinds include butterheads or Bibb lettuces (soft leaves, loose hearts), cos or romaine and semi-cos types (upright, crisp and well-flavoured) and icebergs, Webbs or crispheads (crunchy with dense hearts). Loose-leaf or cut-and-come-again lettuces produce loose masses of small, sometimes coloured, leaves for gathering over a long period.

type Annual crop that prefers cool temperatures. May be grown as a catch- or intercrop. Rotate annually with any group

sowing and planting Sowing to harvest takes about 8–12 weeks, depending on variety and time of year. Sow little and often, especially in summer when heads can deteriorate quickly in heat or drought.

the day before transplanting, and when the new bed is ready, lift the young plants with a fork and carefully separate them.

■ Use a dibber or a broken spade handle to make holes about 15cm (6in) deep at the required spacings and drop a seedling into each after trimming any long roots.

■ Check the plants reach the bottom of the holes and then fill these with water. As the leeks grow their shanks will fill the holes, blanching them at the same time; you can extend the blanch by earthing up plants in early autumn.

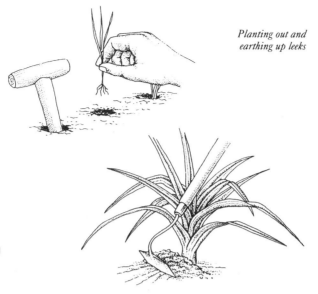

Planting out and earthing up leeks

THINNING FRUIT

A fine warm spring often results in a heavy set of fruit, sometimes more than a tree or bush can support, and you might have to thin the crop while it is still young to avoid broken branches and improve the size and quality of remaining fruits. Gooseberries are the only soft fruit to need thinning: reduce clusters to single berries and pick others so that specimens are left about 5–8cm (2–3in) apart to continue developing into first class dessert berries; the thinnings can be used for cooking. Thin plums to leave perfect fruits 8cm (3in) apart,

peaches and nectarines to single fruits 15cm (6in) apart. With apples and pears, remove the largest fruit in the cluster and any that are misshapen, and then thin to leave a single fruit for every 10–15cm (4–6in) of stem.

MULTIPLYING STRAWBERRIES

As well as producing fruit this month, strawberry plants start to extend long runners that carry tiny plantlets, which root and grow wherever they touch the ground. They are used to replace older crowns after three or four seasons when vigour and yields begin to decline. The first plantlet on

each runner is the strongest but all will develop if you need a lot of plants.

■ Choose the strongest healthy crowns and allow them to make 3–4 plantlets each.

■ Either leave these to root in the ground or peg them on the top of small pots filled with compost; don't forget to water these pots in a dry season.

■ Transplant the young strawberries in late summer to a new bed on well dug and manured soil.

■ If you intend forcing a few plants under glass (see Tasks, p11), pot on the rooted plantlets in 15cm (6in) pots and stand outdoors until needed.

OTHER TASKS

Test if early potatoes are ready; continue earthing up maincrops

Protect ripening soft fruit with nets

Hoe weeds frequently while they are growing strongly

Watch out for aphids arriving in great numbers this month

Thin vegetable seedlings sown in spring

Pinch out the tips of broad beans to deter blackfly

LOOKING AHEAD TO NEXT MONTH

■ Start preparing sites for new strawberry beds and for more winter greens as they become ready for transplanting

■ Prepare a seedbed for sowing spring cabbage

■ Make room in a greenhouse or shed for drying onions, shallots, garlic and bundles of herbs

■ Stock up on green manure seeds for sowing in spare ground as early crops are cleared

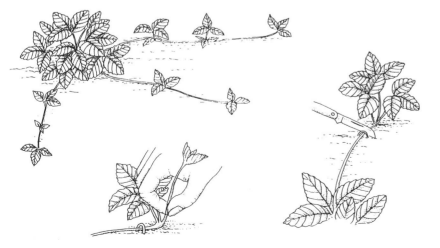

plants
OF THE
month
1

**MAIN CROP ROTATION
GROUPS (see p15)**

1 Legumes, onions
2 Brassicas
3 Root crops

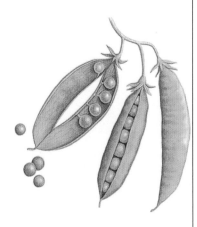

GARDEN PEAS
(Pisum sativum)

An ideal crop for the garden, freshly gathered peas are far superior to the bought product. Round-seeded peas are hardy, those with wrinkled seeds are the sweetest.

type Annual pod-bearing vines, usually needing support and ready for use 12 weeks (early kinds), 15 weeks (maincrop) or 30 weeks (over-wintered) after sowing. Plants vary in height between 45–180cm (1½–6ft). Rotation group 1

sowing and planting Sow in straight drills, either as single rows or in broad drills about 10–15cm (4–6in) wide and containing 3–4 parallel rows of seeds. Sow 5cm (2in) apart and 2.5–5cm (1–2in) deep. Rows should be the same distance apart as the height of the variety. Net sowings to protect them from birds. For early summer harvest sow an early wrinkled variety in early spring, under cloches in cool gardens; alternatively sow under glass, 3–4 seeds per 8cm (3.5in) pot, and plant out complete potfuls 15cm (6in) apart in mid-spring after hardening off. Maincrops are sown *in situ* in mid- and late spring for harvest from mid-summer to early autumn. In early summer sow an early variety again for autumn gathering. In mild districts a hardy round-seeded kind may be sown in late autumn to crop the following spring

site Full sun for early and late crops, light shade for mid-summer crops, and shelter from strong winds. Soils should be free-draining and deeply dug at least a month before sowing, working in plenty of manure or compost to ensure roots do not dry out. Lime soils if they are acid, and rake in a base dressing of general fertiliser when preparing the seedbed

care Hoe between rows, especially in the early stages, and provide plants with support before their first tendrils expand, using twiggy sticks or panels of netting secured to stakes. Earth up the plants when they are about 15cm (6in) high, and mulch with grass clippings to keep the soil moist. In a dry season water occasionally until flowering starts, when plants benefit from a thorough soaking every week until the crop is cleared

harvest Begin picking when pods are well filled and continue every couple of days. Do not leave any pods ungathered as this may depress further flowering. After harvest cut plants down to ground level and compost, leaving the nitrogen-rich roots to decay in the soil

storage Surplus peas are best frozen. Unused pods may be left on the plants to ripen; shell the seeds and keep in airtight tins as dried peas for winter stews or for sowing the following year

pests and diseases Birds and mice often attack seeds and seedlings unless netted. Pea moth is the most common insect pest, laying their eggs in the developing pods which are then found to contain small white grubs; spray plants flowering between early and late summer with insecticide or grow early crops only. In well drained soil mildew on late sowings is likely to be the only serious disease

varieties *Round-seeded:* 'Meteor', 'Pilot'. *Early:* 'Beagle', 'Greenshaft', 'Kelvedon Wonder', 'Little Marvel'. *Maincrop:* 'Alderman', 'Carouby de Mousanne', 'Lynx', 'Markana', 'Onward', 'Sugar Snap'

comments There are several different kinds of maincrop pea. 'Alderman' has long pods containing large seeds, while 'Lynx' is a petit pois producing tiny, very sweet peas. Mangetout peas are grown for their edible pods: 'Carouby de Mousanne' has flat pods, harvested when the peas inside are barely visible, whereas 'Sugar Snap' is a sugar or snow pea with crisp cylindrical pods. Semi-leafless peas such as 'Markana' produce a larger number of tendrils than normal and are self-supporting in sheltered gardens.

   Peas occupy a lot of ground for a relatively small yield. If you are pressed for room concentrate on a few rows of an early variety for harvest in early to mid-summer, or grow a tall variety such as 'Alderman', which will produce up to three times the yield of a short variety in the same space. On a large plot you can sow the same early pea every three weeks from early spring to mid-summer for continuous harvest until mid-autumn

SUMMER CABBAGE
(Brassica oleracea Capitata group*)*

Summer cabbages grow fast to produce dense juicy heads, usually conical and leafy in early maturing kinds whereas later varieties are dense and round with few outer leaves. It is best not to grow a large number, for they mature about the same time as several other popular vegetables such as peas, carrots and beans.

type Biennial usually grown as an annual, in season between late spring and mid-autumn. Rotation group 2

sowing and planting For usable heads in late spring, sow seeds under glass in mid-winter and transplant to pots or modules for hardening off and planting out in early spring. Make further sowings in an outdoor seedbed in early and mid- spring, for transplanting about six weeks later (see spring cabbage, p30). Space transplants 35cm (14in) apart each way for small heads, or 45cm (18in) apart for larger cabbages

site As for spring cabbage (see p30)

care Hoe regularly until their leaves touch and suppress further weed germination. Water whenever necessary to keep the soil consistently moist

harvest Cabbages are ready for use as soon as they are large enough and feel firm. Pull heads as required, cutting off and discarding the roots and outer leaves. Clear crops before the frosts as summer varieties are not hardy

storage Plants are left in the ground until needed

pests and diseases Summer cabbages are subject to the same ailments as other brassicas (see kale, p20), although plants normally grow too fast to be seriously affected by many pests

varieties (In order of maturity) 'Kingspi', 'Hispi', 'Spitfire', 'Greyhound', 'Derby Day', 'Primo 2' ('Golden Acre'), 'Quickstep'

comments Early pointed summer cabbage (the first four listed here) may be cut rather than pulled up, leaving a stump about 8cm (3in) high. Cut a cross 1cm (¹/₂in) deep in the top, hoe a topdressing of general fertiliser around plants and keep them well watered to encourage a second crop of small heads

STRAWBERRY
(*Fragaria* × *ananassa*)

Strawberries give the quickest return of all fruits, and can even bear a crop in their first year. There are three distinct kinds – summer-fruiting, perpetual or remontant, and alpine strawberries – and as all need renewal every few years, plants may be rotated with other crops.

type Low-growing herbaceous perennials, many spreading by means of runners, that can provide fruit from early summer until mid-autumn if several varieties are grown. Rotation group 1, or grow in a separate bed for 3–4 years

sowing and planting Alpines and a few large-fruited varieties can be raised from seed sown under glass in early autumn to fruit the next season, or in mid-winter for light crops late the same year. Sow sparingly in soil-based compost in 8cm (3.5in) pots and cover with a thin layer of grit or vermiculite. Germinate at 18–24°C

(64–75°F), and prick out seedlings when they have two true leaves. Harden off for planting out in late spring

site Warm, sunny sheltered positions give the best flavoured berries. Most fertile, well drained soils are suitable provided they are slightly acid. Dig in plenty of compost or manure, and rake in a base dressing of general fertiliser before planting

care Weed and water regularly. When flowering starts, tuck straw or special mats around each crown to keep the fruit clean, and net rows against birds. Pinch out runners unless needed for propagation, in which case let them root in the ground or peg them down in pots; once rooted (after 4–6 weeks) cut them off and transplant to a fresh site (see Tasks, p65). Strawberries grown as an annual crop are propagated in this way and then discarded after fruiting alternatively renew beds every 3–4 years as quality begins to deteriorate. After fruiting clear the straw from established beds, cut or mow off all foliage and apply a general fertiliser

harvest Gather fruits when fully ripe, complete with their stalks; check every other day. Pick and discard damaged or decaying fruit to avoid spread of disease

storage Surplus fruits can be bottled or turned into preserves; 'Totem' freezes successfully

pests and diseases Dig up and burn stunted plants – large-fruited kinds eventually develop viral diseases and need replacement with new certified stock. Aphids and slugs are common pests; mildew, mould and leaf spot may occur in wet seasons

varieties *Early:* 'Cambridge Vigour', 'Honeoye'. *Mid-season:* 'Elsanta', 'Royal Sovereign', 'Tenira', 'Totem'. *Late:* 'Cambridge Late Pine', 'Doninil'. *Perpetual:* 'Aromel', 'Gento', *Alpine:* 'Alpine Yellow', 'Delicious', 'Fraises des Bois'

comments Most varieties can be forced under glass (see Tasks, p11), while cloches will advance early crops outdoors by about a fortnight and prolong autumn fruting by the same amount. Perpetual strawberries fruit at mid-season and again in the autumn, but if the spring flush of flowers is removed plants crop more heavily from late summer onwards.

Alpine strawberries are small with a distinctive flavour, and crop continuously from mid-summer to late autumn. Plants are compact and make excellent edging; as most kinds are also runnerless, either grow them from seed or divide existing plants in spring. Space alpines 30cm (12in) apart

practical
project
1

HARVEST
SOMETHING
EVERY DAY

CROPS READY IN 12 WEEKS OR LESS

Asparagus peas
Beans *(dwarf French and dwarf runner)*
Beetroot
Cabbage *(Chinese and summer)*
Carrots
Claytonia
Cucumbers *(ridge)*
Kohlrabi
Lettuces *(summer)*
Salad onions (spring sown)
Peas (early)
Radishes
Spinach *(summer)*

Most gardeners prefer to aim for a constant succession of fresh produce from the kitchen garden. Achieving continuity is possible, but avoiding those times when there is nothing, or too much ready for harvest, needs a combination of forward planning and flexibility.

PLANNING FOR CONTINUITY

Many gardeners seem to dig and cultivate for much of the year to supply the kitchen with produce for only about four months. This is perfectly acceptable if you prefer to concentrate on summer vegetables, large quantities of which can grown fast, harvested en masse, and frozen for use during the rest of the year.

By choosing a wider range of crops, however – some of them perennial and others taking many months to mature or being grown primarily for storage – it is possible to have a continuous and varied supply all the year round from an average-size kitchen garden. Flexible planning is essential and you will need to draw up a month-by-month scheme to make the most of available space. Remember to make allowances for weather and other variable factors, using your experience of local influences such as drought, early or late frosts, and exposure to strong or cold winds.

Build your plan around the main crops you would like to grow – plenty of fresh salads, for example, peas and beans in large quantities for freezing or perhaps a range of brassicas for winter use. Check how much space these need and how long they will be there. Try to find other crops that can immediately precede or follow them. Wherever there is a gap between main crops, sow a fast-maturing catch-crop (see p93) or a short-term cover crop of green manure (see p52).

PREPARING FOR A FOLLOW-ON CROP

■ As soon as one vegetable finishes cropping, clear the bed ready for the next.
■ In some cases you can do this before plants are exhausted: Brussels sprout stems still carrying usable buttons, for example, can be pulled up and suspended in a cool shed to allow you to prepare the ground.
■ Some remaining crops can be cleared for freezing or drying, while the last few parsnips and leeks may be dug up and heeled in together elsewhere in the garden to move them out of the way.
■ In spring or autumn the ground can then be dug, and manured where necessary,

before preparing the site for the next crop.

■ In summer, however, it is best not to disturb the soil too deeply, as this will cause rapid drying out; tidy away any crop remains and weeds, hoe or prick over the surface with a fork and break down any clods to a fine tilth if you are sowing the next crop, a little less thoroughly for transplants.

■ Soak the bed if it is dry, and then wait until the next day before raking in a base dressing of general fertiliser, at a rate of about 60g/sq m (2oz/sq yd).

There are many combinations of follow-on crops:

■ Autumn-sown onions lifted in early to mid-summer, for example, make room immediately for transplanted winter cabbages, cleared the following spring in time for you to sow parsnips or carrots.

■ Spring cabbages cleared this month can be followed by marrows, cucumbers, sweetcorn, tomatoes or lettuces, early potatoes by peas, leeks, celery or carrots.

■ Exhausted early peas or overwintered broad beans make way for calabrese and autumn or winter brassicas, while crops cleared in late summer leave room for late leeks, spring cabbages, kale and sprouting broccoli.

SUCCESSIONAL SOWINGS

Apart from main crops sown once in quantity for prolonged or mass harvest, there are others that grow fast and are used while still young: early carrots and peas, baby beets and turnips, summer lettuces, radishes and spinach are perhaps the most popular of these. If too many are grown, unused plants may bolt (run to flower) or deteriorate rapidly in quality, especially during a hot dry summer. Unless you can freeze or otherwise preserve any surplus, it is better to sow small quantities of these at frequent regular intervals, about every 2–3 weeks at the height of the season or soon after seedlings of the previous batch emerge.

There is no need to rotate successional crops during the season unless they have been seriously affected by pests or diseases. Simply clear one batch and weed the bed; topdress with a general fertiliser, hoe and rake level, and then resow. Crops such as kohlrabi, early calabrese and fast-maturing 'greens' can be started in a seedbed, and it is a good idea to reserve space for this at one end of the bed in which older plants are still developing or being harvested, so that you

will have seedlings nearby ready to transplant when the earlier crop is finished.

SEEDLING CROPS

Not all vegetables need to be grown to maturity before they are ready to use. Cut-and-come-again or seedling crops can give a high yield of salad produce very quickly from a small space, and are valuable for making use of ground temporarily vacant and also for harvesting outdoors and under glass before or after main salad crops are available. Spinach, chicory, endive, oriental greens, mustard, cress and lettuces are all suitable for this technique, either separately or in blends known variously as saldisi, mesclun or simply 'salad leaves'.

■ Sow the seeds broadcast at the rate of 12g/sq m (^{1}/₂oz/sq yd) or in parallel drills 10cm (4in) apart; sow sparingly and evenly, or thin seedlings to 2.5cm (1in) apart.

■ The young plants are ready for harvest when they are about 10–15cm (4–6in) tall.

■ Use scissors to cut them down and leave stems 2.5cm (1in) high.

■ The stumps will resprout several times, and by cutting regularly from one end of the bed to the other it is possible to maintain a steady supply for many weeks.

PLANNING CHECKLIST

■ *Make a rough cropping plan for each bed*

■ *Familiarise yourself with the time crops take to mature*

■ *Distinguish between early and maincrop varieties, and grow 2–3 kinds for continuity*

■ *Keep a diary to record sowing, planting and harvest times*

■ *Avoid leaving ground empty for any length of time*

■ *Start follow-on crops in a seedbed and thin or transplant to a nursery bed while they wait for room*

■ *Sow successional crops little and often, repeating sowings as seedlings from the previous batch emerge*

■ *Leave space for intercrops between slow-maturing vegetables*

■ *Use cloches to extend the season by 2–3 weeks at each end*

BEATING THE HUNGRY GAP

A selection of outdoor crops maturing from late winter until the first spring sowings are ready:
Asparagus
Broccoli *(sprouting)*
Brussels sprouts
Cabbage *(spring and savoy)*
Cauliflowers *(overwintered)*
Celeriac
Kale
Landcress
Leeks
Lettuces *(overwintered)*
Rhubarb
Salad seedlings
Spinach
Turnip tops

plants
OF THE
month
2

**MAIN CROP ROTATION
GROUPS (see p15)**

**1 Legumes, onions
2 Brassicas
3 Root crops**

GARLIC
(Allium sativum)

A popular and pungent crop, easily grown in most districts. The bulbs have papery skins enclosing numerous cloves that are used for flavouring and also for medicinal purposes.

type Hardy perennial bulb, normally grown over winter and used all year round fresh or from store. Rotation group 1

planting As garlic needs exposure to low temperatures to produce good crops, spring planting is not always successful and cloves are normally started in mid- to late autumn so that they make a small amount of leaf growth before winter. Carefully break a bulb apart, choosing the plumpest unblemished cloves for planting. Plant each clove, point upwards, in a hole about 10cm (4in) deep on light ground, half that depth on clay, and cover with soil. Space cloves 20cm (8in) apart each way, or every 10cm (4in) in rows 30cm (12in) apart. In very cold areas or on wet soils, plant individually in 11cm (4in) pots and keep in a coldframe until spring when they can be transplanted outdoors

site Full sun outdoors or under glass where summers are cool. The best bulbs grow on light, well drained soils that are moderately fertile. Work plenty of grit and coarse compost into heavy ground or grow bulbs in a raised bed

care Water occasionally in dry weather and keep plants weed free

harvest Bulbs start ripening at mid-summer, when plants may be dug up for immediate use. After a few weeks, when 5–6 leaves turn yellow, the whole crop should be lifted – do not wait until the top growth is completely dead. Fork up the plants carefully and suspend in bunches in full sun or under glass

storage When the skins are dry and papery, gently rub bulbs clean and plait them together or hang up in bundles in a dry place, ideally in a temperature of 5–10°C (41–50°F). They will keep sound until the following spring or early summer

**pests
and
diseases** Garlic is subject to the same ailments as onions (see p90), but in good soils these are rarely a problem

varieties Various selections are listed in catalogues, but differences between them are slight. Where possible buy from a reputable supplier offering bulbs grown in the same climate. Cloves from your own crop may be saved for replanting if healthy, but avoid imported bulbs sold for consumption as these are often infected with viral diseases

comments Elephant or jumbo garlic has enormous, mildly flavoured bulbs grown in the same way. All kinds may produce 'flower'-heads of tiny bulblets or 'pips', and small offsets below ground; the main bulbs are still usable, while the pips and offsets can be sown in a seedbed where they will make small bulbs for planting the following year

POTATO
(Solanum tuberosum)

A productive vegetable often used as a pioneer crop on fresh ground, where the preparation and later care helps to cultivate the soil for other crops. Early varieties are the most popular and the first harvested; maincrops produce the heaviest yields if you have room to grow them, and can be stored for winter use.

type Herbaceous perennial with underground tubers. Rotation group 3, or may be grown as an extra group 4 in a 4-year rotation

**sowing
and
planting** Potatoes are grown from small tubers, perhaps saved from a previous healthy crop but preferably bought as seed potatoes or sets that are certified disease free. Buy them at least 6 weeks before planting and lay them out immediately to 'chit' (see Tasks, p10). Plant early varieties in early to mid-spring, under cloches in cold gardens, following with maincrops 3–4 weeks later. Plant sets 10–15cm (4–6in) deep in drills or individual holes made with a dibber. Space earlies every 30cm (12in) in rows 45cm (18in) apart, other kinds at 38cm (15in) in rows 60cm (24in) apart. Cover the tubers with soil to leave a slight ridge

site Open, sunny positions, free from late spring frosts. Most well drained soils are suitable and will produce a worthwhile crop, but any compost or manure that can be added before planting will greatly increase yields. Avoid recently limed soils. A fortnight before planting give the area a base dressing of general fertiliser

care In the event of frost protect the young growth with newspapers or straw, or draw a little soil over it. Earth up plants to shield the tubers from light, which turns them green and inedible. When top growth is about 23cm (9in) high, hoe both sides of the row and bank some of this loose soil around plants to form a ridge halfway up the stems. Once is sufficient for earlies, but maincrops need earthing up every 2–3 weeks until the leaves of adjacent rows meet. Consistent moisture is important for earlies to make strong growth, so water regularly in dry weather; water maincrops heavily once or twice after flowering begins

harvest Early varieties are usually ready 12–15 weeks after planting, when their flowers are fully open. Test by scraping a little soil from the side of the ridge – if any tubers have reached the size of a hen's egg you can start lifting. Use a fork inserted well away from stems to avoid damaging tubers, grasp the stems and ease the whole plant from the soil; check you have unearthed all the tubers before moving on to the next plant. Maincrops are ready when the foliage turns brown in autumn; cut down the stems and wait another fortnight before lifting the whole crop

storage Earlies are normally dug as required, but maincrops are grown for storing. Lift on a fine day and leave the tubers on the surface to dry for a few hours. Reserve any that are damaged for immediate use, and pack the rest in paper sacks or wooden boxes for storing in a dry, dark place free from frost

pests and diseases Various soil pests, such as cutworms and slugs, like potatoes, although some varieties are less attractive than others; wireworms may be a problem on freshly dug grassland. Most diseases can be prevented by good husbandry and by using bought sets certified free from viruses. Spray heavy infestations of aphids, as these spread diseases; watch out for potato blight on maincrops from early summer onwards, and spray with copper fungicide if symptoms appear

varieties *Early:* 'Accent', 'Arran Pilot', 'Concorde', 'Foremost', 'Maris Bard', 'Pentland Javelin'. *Maincrop:* 'Cara', 'Kondor', 'Marfona', 'Maris Piper', 'Pentland Squire', 'Romano', 'Sante'

comments Many more varieties are available, all worth growing. Modern kinds tend to be resistant to certain diseases ('Sante' to blight, for example) or pests (slugs rarely bother 'Pentland Squire'). Check your soil type, as some are more suitable than others for light soils prone to drought or for clay. Varieties classed as second earlies behave as maincrops but may be ready for lifting from mid- to late summer. All kinds may be grown under black polythene sheeting (see p80), which avoids the need for earthing up

MINT

(Mentha species)

Many different kinds of mint are grown in gardens, but the most popular for culinary use are apple- or round-leaved-mint *(Mentha rotundifolia)*, peppermint *(M. × piperita)* and spearmint *(M. spicata).*

type Hardy herbaceous perennials with aromatic foliage, spreading by underground runners. Height is generally about 60cm (2ft), but shorter and prostrate mints also grown

sowing and planting Mint can be grown from seed, sown in pots under glass in spring, and existing plants often self-seed, producing hybrids if several types are grown together. Usually pot-grown plants are bought and planted about 15–23cm (6–9in) apart in early to mid-spring; alternatively pieces of root from healthy plants are laid horizontally 5cm (2in) deep and the same distance apart

site Full sun or light shade, in rich soil that is moist and weed free. Dig the site thoroughly and work in compost or manure

care Water freely until established; thereafter mint needs little care. Cut down some of the stems at mid-summer to stimulate a supply of young foliage for use late in the season. Cut down dead stems in autumn and topdress plants with a little bonemeal. Mints tend to spread freely and exhaust the soil, so remake beds every 3–4 years, digging up and dividing plants in autumn and replanting on a fresh site

harvest Gather the fresh tips of shoots as required between late spring and the first frosts. A few roots may be dug up in mid-autumn and replanted in deep pots or boxes of garden soil to overwinter under glass and cut in early spring

storage Mint may be frozen or dried for winter use. Cut stems in summer and hang them up until brittle enough to crumble; for freezing, pick leaves and store whole in a plastic bag or chop and pack in water in ice-cube trays. Mint can also be preserved in oil, syrup or vinegar

pests and diseases Plants are seldom troubled by pests, but mint rust may be a serious problem, disfiguring leaves with orange or black postules and causing eventual dieback. Either burn infected foliage with a flame gun and scorch the soil to kill the spores, or dig up and burn plants and start again elsewhere with fresh stock

comments Because they are invasive, mints are often grown in containers, or in an old bottomless bucket or box buried in the ground. Apart from the common culinary forms, there are many other mints worth growing in the kitchen garden, many of them with unusual flavours or leaf colours. Prostrate kinds such as pennyroyal and Corsican mint are ideal for edging beds and paths

practical
project
2

WATERING YOUR
GARDEN

USING GREY WATER
As much water leaves a house as goes into it. Grey water is water that has been used for bathing or washing, and this is useful for irrigation, especially when mains water restrictions are in force. Environmentally aware gardeners divert grey water into garden pools or storage tanks planted with reeds to filter out unwanted chemicals and detergents, but under normal conditions it is quite safe to collect and use untreated grey water for irrigating crops.

A ready supply of water is the most important of the factors essential for plant growth. Knowing how much water to give, and when, depends on a number of variables, including your type of soil and the crops you cultivate.

THE SOIL RESERVOIR

Water needs to be available whenever plants are in active growth. Stems and leaves depend on the water pressure inside the plant to keep them firm, while the roots can only absorb food substances when these are dissolved in water. This is why growth stops and plants wilt during a drought. For most of the year there is enough water in the ground to meet these needs, but the amount that can be stored is governed by the nature and texture of the soil.

Water is held in the soil partly by humus, the spongy remains of partly-decayed organic matter, and also as a thin film coating the soil particles. Clay has fine particles with a large total surface area, and can therefore absorb a lot of water (three times as much as sandy soil) but tends to be reluctant to release it – the reason why clay soils take a long time to warm up and dry out in the spring. Light soil, on the other hand, is soon saturated but dries very quickly.

During the active growing season, demands on the soil reservoir increase. To keep levels topped up in summer requires about 2.5cm (1in) of rainfall every 7–10 days according to the type of soil. As this rarely occurs in an average year, watering eventually becomes necessary to maintain healthy growth, especially of those plants at

particular risk. The critical decision for most gardeners is when to start and how much to give.

HOW TO DELAY WATERING

There is no virtue in starting to water too soon, as this may cause waterlogging or stimulate the growth of shallow roots that later suffer in dry weather. You can postpone the need to irrigate by improving the water retentiveness of the soil.

Organic material such as compost and manure benefits all soils. It slows down drainage and evaporation from sandy soils and opens up clay to help release stored water and allow roots to search more easily for it. Frequent hoeing was once thought to reduce evaporation by creating a surface barrier or 'dust mulch' of fine dry soil, but mulching with other materials is more efficient (see Tasks, p53). Plants themselves can reduce water loss by shading the bare soil surface, and close planting to achieve rapid ground cover is a useful precaution on naturally dry soils, especially if weeds are also firmly controlled to eliminate competition for water. Underplanting sweetcorn, Brussels sprouts and similar widely spaced plants with groundcover crops such as marrows, asparagus peas or New Zealand spinach is an alternative way to keep the soil surface protected.

TARGETING CROPS

When watering becomes inevitable, concentrate on the most urgent areas. Watering the whole garden indiscriminately is both time-consuming and wasteful, since many crops need it only during certain stages of growth. Research into the precise needs of plants has revealed, for example, that early potatoes crop best if kept consistently moist throughout growth, whereas maincrops benefit most with one or two heavy soakings when the young tubers are the size of marbles, normally when flowering starts.

Crops that you should keep consistently moist include all leafy vegetables such as brassicas, lettuces and spinach (because water generally encourages leaf growth), together with all seedlings, newly planted or transplanted crops, those in shallow soils and containers, and any growing close to walls. Root vegetables should be kept just moist

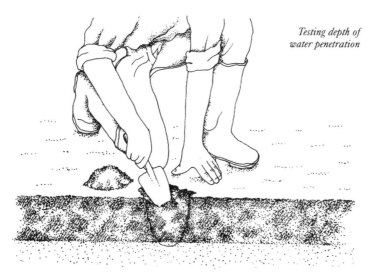

Testing depth of water penetration

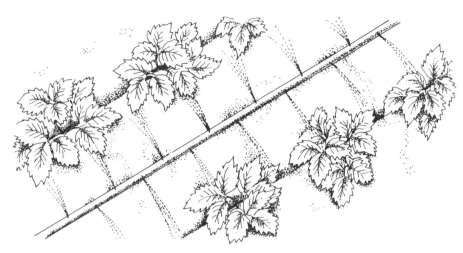

enough to encourage active growth without excessive foliage, while crops that produce seeds and fruits (peas, beans, tomatoes, sweetcorn) need plenty of water at flowering time and while their fruits are swelling.

Ideal amounts have been measured precisely and vary to a bewildering extent. As a rule of thumb, avoid giving small quantities that merely dampen the surface; heavy waterings of not less than about 5 litres/sq m (1 gal/sq yd) – weekly on light soils or every 10–14 days on clay – are more beneficial to growing plants, with double that rate at critical stages. Never let the soil dry out altogether, and do not suddenly soak root or fruit crops after a period of drought as this can cause cracking. Remember, though, that restricting water slightly can improve the flavour of crops such as tomatoes and carrots.

WATERING EQUIPMENT

For small areas and individual plants, there is nothing more efficient than a watering can, fitted with a fine rose for seedbeds and seedlings. On a larger scale a hosepipe saves time and effort – check with your water authority about the need for a hosepipe licence and for a non-return valve which is coupled between the hose and the tap to prevent water from siphoning back into the mains.

Watering manually with a hose can become tedious, with the result that plants often get less than they need. Variable oscillating sprinklers solve this problem but need to be finely adjustable, both to regulate the area covered and to set the density of the spray: a fine mist will drift away rather than penetrate the soil, while a coarse spray of large drops will beat a hard cap on the surface so that much of the water runs to waste. Automatic devices are available that monitor and shut off the flow of water after a given time or volume.

Perforated tubing may be laid on the ground between rows of plants, either to deliver a concentrated band of spray (sprinkler pipes, spray lines) or to water plants gently at ground level (permeable hose, seep hose). You can either move them from one bed to another in rotation or leave them permanently in place; some kinds of seep hoses are intended to be buried a short distance below the surface for the duration of the season.

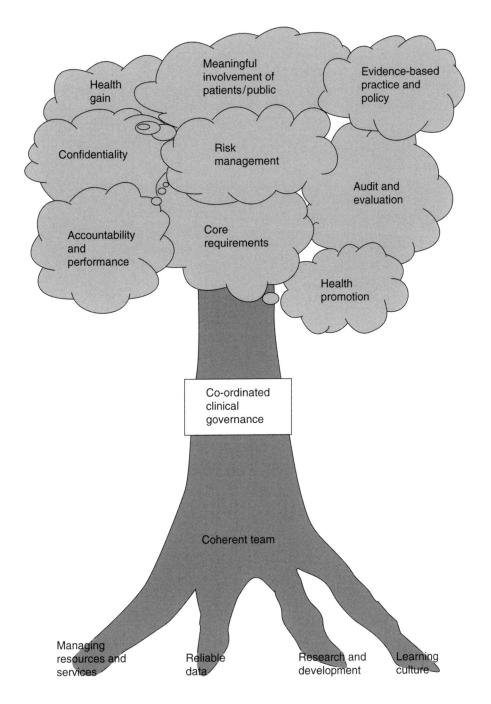

Figure A   'Routes' and branches of clinical governance.

PART ONE

Introduction

CHAPTER ONE

What is clinical governance and how does it fit with professional and service development?

Clinical governance underpins professional and service development. Clinical governance 'is doing anything and everything required to maximise quality'.[1] It is about finding ways to 'implement care that works in an environment in which clinical effectiveness can flourish by establishing a facilitatory culture'.[2]

The emphasis is on education and training programmes being relevant to service needs, whether at organisational or individual levels. 'Continuing professional development (CPD) programmes need to meet both the learning needs of individual health professionals to inspire public confidence in their skills ... and the wider service development needs of the NHS'.[3] CPD is not just what you *want* to do, but what you *need* to do.

Lifelong learning and CPD are integral to the concept of clinical governance. Everyone should have learning goals that are relevant to service development. We have identified the following 14 themes as core components of professional and service development which, taken together, constitute clinical governance. These are:

- Learning culture: in your practice, the PCG/PCT, the trust and the NHS at large.
- Research and development culture: throughout the NHS.
- Reliable data: in your practice or trust, PCG/PCT, the NHS as a seamless whole.
- Well-managed resources and services, as individuals, as a team, as a practice, across the NHS and in conjunction with social care and local authorities.
- Coherent team: well-integrated teams within your practice or trust or PCG/PCT.
- Meaningful involvement of patients and the public: in your practice, PCG/PCT and the NHS.

- Health gain: activities to improve the health of patients served by your practice and through different geographical areas of the NHS.
- Confidentiality: of information in consultations, in medical notes, between practitioners.
- Evidence-based practice and policy: applying it in practice, in the PCG/PCT, across the trust or the NHS.
- Accountability and performance: for standards, performance of individuals, the practice or trust, the PCG/PCT and the NHS – to the public and those in authority.
- Core requirements: good fit between skill mix and competence, communication, workforce numbers, morale in general practices and across the PCG/PCT.
- Health promotion: for patients, the public – targeting those with most needs.
- Audit and evaluation: when making changes; of individuals' and practices' or a trust's performance, of practice or PCG/PCT achievements and district services.
- Risk management: proactive review, follow-up, risk management, risk reduction.

The aims of the government's programme of modernisation of the health services are to:[3]

- tackle the causes of ill health
- make services convenient, quick and easy to use
- ensure the consistency of services regardless of where you live
- try and provide 'joined up' services that are not constrained by artificial barriers between services, such as health and social services
- invest in improving the workforce and infrastructure.[1]

through:[4]

- clear national standards set by the National Service Frameworks (NSFs) and National Institute of Clinical Excellence (NICE)
- local delivery of quality services
- monitoring of services through the Commission for Health Improvement (CHI)
- consultation with patients and the public.

Clinical governance is relevant to all five aims and integral to the delivery of high-quality services in consultation with patients and the public at large. Minimising inequalities is at the heart of clinical governance:

- as inequalities in healthcare: variations in access, service provision or standards of care and discrimination on the grounds of age, gender, ethnicity, sexuality, disability, etc.
- as inequalities of people's health: influenced by risky lifestyles and social determinants of health such as poor housing, low income, transport.

The components of clinical governance are not new. Bringing them together under the banner of clinical governance and introducing more explicit accountability for perform-ance is a new style of working. The reception given to clinical governance has ranged from an enthusiastic welcome[5] to the cautious warning that 'there is no evidence only presumption, that these innovations will improve quality, and they may increase rather than decrease costs'.[6] Carefully evaluating your work and subsequent improvements in patient care will enable you to form your own view about the place of clinical governance.

---

individual personal development plans

will feed into a

workplace- or practice-based professional development plan

that will feed into

the organisation's business plan; all underpinned by clinical governance

---

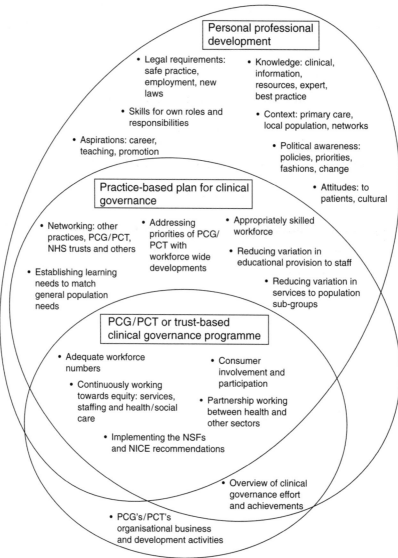

Note: The topics given as priority areas for development are examples and not intended to constitute comprehensive lists.

Figure 1.1 How do the components of professional development fit with clinical governance in your practice and your PCG/PCT or other NHS trust?

CHAPTER TWO

How to do it: identify your service development needs and your associated learning needs

Get organised as an individual

1   Make your overall learning and development plan. You'll need to consider the study time needed, commitment, both your own and wider NHS perspectives, motivation, prioritisation and support. Consider your own plan as contributing to the wider workplace-based clinical governance programme.

2   Identify your learning and service development needs. Find the balance between your needs as an individual and your working environment (systems and procedures in your practice, the PCG/PCT, the NHS as a whole).

3   Devise a programme that meets your learning and service development needs and fits with the priorities of your practice or trust.

4   Select the educational material, making it happen in your practice.

5   Appraise your own learning and development, and what you have achieved in improvements to patient care. Get feedback from others. Demonstrate that you are fit to practise.

6   Review the fit between you and your practice or your trust; demonstrate that your working environment is fit for you to practise from.

7   Identify new areas of learning and development from your evaluation of how you are doing. Anticipate your needs if your circumstances are about to change for you or your working environment.

Get organised as a practice or workplace team

1   Start with the business plan of your practice or trust. If there is no business plan, consider drawing one up. What are the main areas of service development for the forthcoming year, or, looking ahead, the next three years? The plan should include important NHS priorities such as:

  • those in the local health improvement programme (HImP)
  • recent or expected NSFs
  • local priorities such as the conditions for which there are higher than average death rates in your local population
  • current or anticipated changes in your service delivery, such as if you are developing new models of care with integrated nursing teams.

2   Identify service development needs and staff learning needs using some of the range of methods that follow in the next section. What are the main areas of planned development for which you and other staff will need new knowledge and skills? Consider checking with others from outside the practice whether you have got it right. You might ask patients, the public (i.e. non-users of your services), others in the local trust, PCG/PCT, local tutors, etc. Define:

  • short-term objectives for learning and service development for the next year
  • medium-term objectives for up to three years.

3   Identify what staff need to learn to be able to deliver your clinical governance development programme. Balance clinical and non-clinical needs between individuals and their working environment (systems and procedures in the practice, the PCG/PCT or trust, the NHS as a whole). This will include:

  • generic learning that is relevant for everyone, e.g. communication
  • team building
  • specific skills for the particular roles and responsibilities of all included in the workplace-based plan.

4   Assess the infrastructure required to deliver your planned clinical governance programme and identify from where you will obtain the necessary resources.

5   When making your overall clinical governance plan you'll need to consider:

  • which staff it covers: doctors, nurses, therapists and non-clinical staff; does it also include your cleaners, psychologists, community pharmacists, attached staff and patients?
  • the extent and resource costs for service developments and learning: actual costs to individuals, the practice; include opportunity costs
  • the extent of the commitment of the organisation and staff
  • the perspectives of your staff, the organisation as a whole, the PCG/PCT or trust, the district and the wider NHS (as in Figure 1.1)

- how to motivate the staff
- how to prioritise development between topics, between different services or practices and between staff
- how to support the staff through changes
- how to evaluate what has been achieved
- how to assess and meet learning and service development needs as they occur.

Give each member of staff a definite role and responsibility in the overall plan. Think how and by whom the learning and clinical governance effort will be evaluated and achievements monitored; how and by whom new learning needs will be identified and included.

6   Make it happen in practice.

7   Demonstrate that your working environment is fit for the staff to practise in, with good records of what you have achieved: for example, improvements to the quality of patient care, staff wellbeing, effective systems, staff development.

8   Evaluate the extent and quality of the service developments and associated learning; and describe what has still to be addressed.

CHAPTER THREE

Use a range of methods to identify your service development and learning needs

See Module 1 Establishing and sustaining a learning culture.

Determine what it is that you 'don't know you don't know' by:

- asking patients, users and non-users of your service
- comparing your performance against best practice
- comparing your performance against objectives in business plans or national directives
- asking colleagues from different disciplines about shortfalls in how your work interfaces with theirs.

Try to use several different methods of identifying service development and learning needs for each of the 14 themes that you focus on, so that you get a rounded picture. To start with, select the two, three or four themes that are key priorities for your situation.

Look at this range of methods for identifying your service development and learning needs. Use any or a mix of all of these methods.

1 Appraise yourself – review how you and your colleagues work. Write down any specific needs that you think you or colleagues have.

Your and your practice's or PCG/PCT's or trust's aspirations for:
- new models of service delivery

- new roles or responsibilities in the organisation
- your organisation's vision for change.

Your attitudes to:
- other disciplines
- patients
- lifelong learning
- culture
- change.

Context of work:
- networking in health and non-health settings
- team relationships
- different subgroups of the population
- historical service provision
- the organisation's priorities.

Your knowledge:
- clinical
- about your local population
- of best practice
- range of services available locally
- about your organisation
- local experts or other provision
- systems and procedures in your organisation
- inequalities of health or healthcare of your patient population.

Legal requirements:
- health and safety at work
- new legislation
- employment procedures, e.g. equal opportunities
- safe practices, e.g. personal safety.

Awareness of health policies:
- new health policies
- national priorities
- local priorities, e.g. HImP
- fashions, e.g. in clinical practice or how education is delivered.

Skills:
- team working and communication
- effective working practices
- your basic competence
- health needs assessment
- communication between trusts and PCGs/PCTs
- organisational development of your team

- information technology and computer capability
- your specialist areas
- planning.

2 Ask other people what they think of you: gain feedback from colleagues

Workshops, individual mentoring, small groups or just talking with colleagues about how you do your job all help you to assess your needs.

Unless you have some method of recording what you need to learn (or think) about, you will easily forget it in the busy life that you lead. Identifying and using problems that arise naturally in the course of your work help to make it relevant.

> Notebooks, a personal portfolio, a diary or more formal files (paper or computer) help to organise your learning and that of your team.

3 Select an audit (*see* Module 9 Audit and evaluation)

Set standards for your performance and compare them to best practice, make changes and re-audit. Choose a topic where changes will make a significant difference to patient care.

- Case note analysis: provides an insight into current recorded practice.
- Peer review: compare an area of work with that of another individual or compare work teams.
- Criteria-based audit: compares clinical practice with specific standards, guidelines or protocols. Re-audit of changes should demonstrate improvements in the quality of care.

> Audit your care of diabetic patients by comparing the proportion of patients meeting your criteria for good diabetic care over intervals of time. Consult with all those involved – the patients and carers, chiropodists, nurses, doctors, reception staff, pharmacists, etc. District nurses and health visitors need to be involved with the hard-to-reach groups such as the housebound. Decide how you could improve what you do, put it into action and then re-audit.

- External audit: audit facilitators, managers, etc., may have data on indicators of your performance; involve your colleagues in using the information in an audit capacity.

- Direct observation: record what is observed for later action – make a note now before you forget.
- Surveys: you might carry out a survey as a general indicator of care or for detecting a problem rather than as an accurate measurement of performance.
- Tracer criteria: assessing the quality of care of a tracer condition may be used to represent the quality of care of other similar conditions or more complex problems. Tracer criteria should be easily defined and measured.

Audit the care of incontinence of the residents in a nursing home as an indicator of the general quality of care.

- Significant event audit: think of a critical incident where a patient or you experienced an adverse event.

▼

Steps of a significant event audit

- Step 1: Describe the critical incident – who, what, when.
- Step 2: Recount the effects of the event on the participants and the professionals involved.
- Step 3: Deduce the reasons for the critical event or situation arising, through discussion with other colleagues, review of case notes or other records.
- Step 4: Decide how you or others might have behaved differently and describe your options for how the procedures at work might be changed to reduce or eliminate reoccurrence.
- Step 5: Agree any changes that are needed, how they will be implemented, who will be responsible for what and when.
- Step 6: Re-audit at a later date to see whether changes to procedures are having the desired effects. Give feedback to the practice team. Acknowledge good care.

4 Monitor your or your practice's or trust's clinical care

- Use prescribing and cost data.

> Review the extent to which you adhere to pre-agreed clinical protocols, guidelines and care pathways. Does being unable to justify deviations from the agreed procedures reveal any learning or service development needs?

- Identify shortfalls in the provision of care and services; use computer searches.

5 Monitor access, availability, satisfaction

- Access and availability.

> You could look at waiting times to see a health professional in a clinic by using:
>
> - computerised appointment lists or paper and pen to record the time of arrival, the time of the appointment, the time seen
> - next available appointments, which can easily be monitored by computer, or more painfully by manual searches of the appointment books
> - data to find out whether patients are being prioritised according to pre-agreed criteria for referral.
>
> Compare the results at intervals and use as a motivator for change if necessary.

- Patient satisfaction: patient satisfaction surveys may seem cheap and easy but their shortcomings may outweigh their usefulness. Suggestion boxes may be useful or try keeping a complete record of all suggestions and complaints from patients, however trivial, looking for patterns in the comments received.
- Referrals to other agencies and hospitals: you can audit whether referrals are appropriate by the use of proformas or templates.

6 Monitoring systems and procedures

Regular problems need action and reviews. Regular team meetings can flag up such problems at an early stage.

If a problem is not solved the first time then look at it another way. You may need to seek more information before planning action. Monitoring systems need to be in place for all equipment. Make sure that there is good data recording of the purchase, arrangements for servicing and responsibility for maintenance and checking (with deputy arrangements in case of absence or sickness). Staff health records need to be checked as well and robust systems put into place. Be especially careful when employing locum or temporary staff or with initial employment.

7 Informal conversations – in the corridor, over coffee

It is often said that people learn most on courses when chatting with colleagues at the coffee and meal breaks. This is when you realise that other people are doing things differently from you – and if they seem to be doing it better and achieving more, you can challenge yourself to decide if this matter could be one of your blind spots.

8 Strengths, weaknesses, opportunities and threats (SWOT) analysis

Undertake a SWOT analysis of your own performance or that of your workplace team or organisation, on your own, or with a workmate or mentor, or with a group of colleagues.

Strengths and weaknesses of individual practitioners might include:

- knowledge
- experience
- expertise
- research skills
- inter-professional relationships
- communication skills
- political skills

- organisational skills
- decision making
- timekeeping
- teaching skills.

Strengths and weaknesses of the practice organisation might relate to most of these aspects too as well as resources – staff, skills, structural.

Opportunities might relate to unexploited potential strengths, expected changes, options for career development pathways, hobbies and interests that might usefully be expanded.

Threats will include factors and circumstances that prevent you from achieving your aims for personal, professional and practice development.

Prioritise important factors. Draw up goals and a timed action plan.

9 Compare your performance (*see* Module 13 Accountability and performance)

There are many assessment programmes with externally set criteria and standards. Standards may be relative, that is referenced to norms, or absolute, that is referenced to criteria.

You could compare your performance against external criteria for: clinical practice; record keeping; access and availability; emergency treatments; professional–patient relationships; effective use of resources; handling mistakes or complaints.

10 Observation of your work environment and role

Look at the equipment in your workplace. Do you know how to operate it properly?

Analyse all the various roles and responsibilities of your current posts. Are you capable of fulfilling these? Do you know what other colleagues do or how their roles and responsibilities interface with yours? Ask others what they think of your performance. You could ask someone to observe you at work and feed back their opinions in a constructive discussion; then you could repay the favour by reviewing them at work.

11 Reading and reflecting

Try to read articles in respected journals regularly. Actively reflect[7] on what the key relevant messages mean for you.

12 Educational appraisal

Discuss in a formal way your performance, job situation and learning needs with a colleague, clinical tutor or clinical supervisor. You might make a timed action plan for learning as a result.

13 Review the business or development plan of your practice or PCG/PCT or trust and other official strategic documents or directives

Do you know the contents of all the official and informal strategic documents that are relevant to your work? If so, are you aware of the implications for you and your work? Note down any gaps and whether you have any associated learning needs.

14 Job appraisal

Good employment practice includes regular job appraisal, e.g. annually. This gives you an opportunity to review how well you are doing in your own view and that of the person who is appraising you. Identify your learning needs and how they will be met in the context of your current job or by agreed changes to your roles and responsibilities.

If you are a senior manager or doctor you might undertake peer appraisal with another senior colleague whom you trust and whose opinion you respect.

CHAPTER FOUR

Where do you want to be and how do you get there?

Having found out where you are at present, you have to decide where you want to be next before making a plan for clinical governance in your practice or PCG/PCT or trust.

▼

From the practice or PCG/PCT or trust perspective

Aspiration	Destination example	Route – to your priorities
Organisation's vision for change	Practice provides XXX services for the PCG/PCT or trust	Training and expertise in XXX; links to secondary care; bid for equipment; support services; accommodation; staffing time
	Patients to be able to access the health visitor for advice more easily	Time set aside for telephone consultations, training and computer assistance software programme
	Complete audit cycles regularly	Incorporate audit into regular work; training; invest in information technology (IT) so it is automatic; set up regular reviews and time for staff to undertake relevant audits
	Set up and run regular multidisciplinary meetings	Someone to organise it; protected time for the staff to attend; IT support and access
	Improve implementation of evidence-based medicine and nursing	Training; education; research involvement; clinical meetings; audit and review procedures that are trust-, practice- or PCG/PCT-based; protected time for activities
	Improve the management of complaints	Training for the complaints manager and relevant staff; systematic review of complaints procedures; comparison with others in the practice or PCG/PCT or trust
	Monitor standards of practice nursing	Training in review, clinical supervision and systematic audit procedures; rectify substandard practice at individual and team levels; training and education
	Develop occupational health services for the staff	PCG/PCT or trust to set aside funds for development and employment of suitable personnel
	Improvement of access to clinical records	Standardisation of entry data; IT training; new equipment; compare standards in practice across PCG/PCT or trust

Now have a go at shaping the vision for your clinical governance plan.

From the practice or PCG/PCT or trust perspective

Aspiration	*Destination*	*Route – to your priorities*
Organisation's vision for change		

CHAPTER FIVE

Setting priorities for developing clinical governance

You and your colleagues will have been able to make a wish list after following the previous stages on needs assessment. Select those topics that are tied into organisational priorities, have clear aims and objectives, and are achievable within your time and resource constraints. Collect information from all the team, the patients, users and carers to feed back before you make decisions on how to progress. Remember to take external influences into account such as the NSFs, governmental priorities, the district priorities in the HImP, NICE, etc.

When ranking topics in order of priority consider whether:

- the project aims and objectives are clearly defined
- the topic is important:
  - for the population served (e.g. the size of the problem and/or its severity)
  or
  - for the individual/team skills, knowledge or attitudes
- it is feasible
- it is affordable
- it will make enough difference
- it fits in with other priorities.

You will still have more ideas than can possibly be implemented. Remember the highest priority – the health service is for patients who use it or who will do so in the future. Imagine that your primary care team, PCG/PCT, trust or you as an individual run a picture gallery. You have been sent a large number of pictures and exhibits. You want the critics to acclaim the pictures on display. You need to convince others of your wisdom, common sense and business acumen. You would not want everyone who has sent in a picture to decide on whose picture should be hung, so you set up a 'Hanging Committee'.

Who should be on your 'Hanging Committee' to decide which of the topics on your lists of aspirations should be prioritised? It has to be representative and not autocratic or idiosyncratic. Look at the 'routes and branches' of the clinical governance tree. You will need people to represent each root, trunk and branch.

Set dates for completion of the various stages. How will you set standards and evaluate what you have done? You might want to use a table as in the example below.

Table 5.1 Improve the management of scabies by increasing self-management by patients: timetabled action plan

	May 00	August	Nov	Feb 01
Search for number of prescriptions		→		
Literature and resource search for best practice	→			
Patient focus group to discover patients' ideas		→		
Poster and leaflet campaign			→	
Interdisciplinary working with school nurses			→	
Interdisciplinary working with pharmacists			→	
Repeat search for number of prescriptions				→

Template for your practice- or workplace-based clinical governance plan
Photocopy the three pages and complete one chart per priority topic

The topic:
Who chose it?
How was the choice made?

Justify why topic is a priority:
a trust or practice priority?
a district priority?
a national priority?

Who will be included in the plan? (give posts and names of doctors, nurses, therapists, managers, non-clinical staff, others from outside the practice, patients)

Who will collect the baseline information and how?

Where are you now? (baseline)

What information will you obtain about individual learning wishes and needs?
How will you obtain this and who will do it: self-completion checklists, discussion, appraisal, patient feedback?

What are the service development and associated learning needs for the PCG/ PCT or trust or practice and how do they match the needs of individuals?

How will you prioritise everyone's needs in a fair and open way?

Patients' or the public input to your plan.

Action plan (include objectives, timetabled action, expected outcomes)

How does your clinical governance plan tie in with your other strategic plans?
(for example the practice's or trust's business or development plan, the Primary Care
Investment Plan?)

What additional resources will you require to execute your plan and from where do
you hope to obtain them? (will staff have to pay any course fees or undertake learning in
their own time?)

**How much protected time will you allocate to staff to undertake the learning
described in your plan?**

How will you evaluate your learning plan? (who will be responsible for what?)

How will you know when you have achieved your objectives? (how will you measure
success?)

How will you handle new learning requirements as they crop up?

CHAPTER SIX

You have identified your learning needs – now what?

Using the modules to your advantage

Most of what you will need to know as a health professional or manager who wants to provide high-quality healthcare that is patient-centred and relevant to service needs, follows on here. We have arranged the material as individual modules around the 14 themes of clinical governance.

The front page of each module summarises the topics contained within it. You might want to pick one or two topics from each of the 14 modules, or work through all the topics of one or two modules. The type and number of topics or modules will depend on what learning needs you have identified from the work you have done up to this point. And it will depend on whether you are using this programme to devise your own personal or professional development plan, or are working as a practice team on one or more agreed priority areas.

At the end of each module is:

- a personal learning record for you to complete
- **an action plan in which to describe how you will meet your learning needs with respect to the module**
- an evaluation chart to record what has been achieved and what education and work is still outstanding.

These record charts have been drawn up in such a way that you can complete them from your own individual perspective, or as a team or organisation (your practice, your PCG/PCT or trust). GPs, nurses, therapists and practice managers who have tried out these charts found them easy to use and found that they encouraged them to adopt a more structured approach to learning and improving.

If you are working on your own you will need to be firm with yourself about keeping to the times set out in your action plans and making changes in your everyday practice. Discussing progress with a local tutor or colleague might encourage you to keep on track and make sure that you are keeping a balanced perspective on developments.

Use the same tools to evaluate your progress as you used to identify your learning needs – refer back to the variety of methods described earlier in the book.

CHAPTER SEVEN

Baseline review

Your practice or workplace

Start collecting evidence about structures and activities in the practice that show you are taking clinical governance seriously. You might undertake an annual review with quarterly progress reports.

1 Structures

- Your medical records – paper or electronic – can you demonstrate whether they are accurate, summarised, up to date? What are the access arrangements; how secure are they? To what extent are diseases coded for computer entry?
- Computer system and its capability – is it set up for routine searches of patient data?
- Equipment – to provide high-quality primary care. Are nebulisers, a defibrillator, a spirometer, sphygmomanometers in good working order? Do you have an electro-cardiogram (ECG) machine and can the practice nurse operate it?

2 Leadership

- Is there a clinical governance lead; does he or she lead on prescribing too? Does some-one else lead on education? How do the practice manager's roles and responsibilities interface with those of these other leads?

3 Baseline assessment of current performance

- You will be using a variety of the methods described in this book to demonstrate your current performance in a range of key priority areas; with associated action plans for improvement.
- Your educational activities – hopefully activities tied into a practice-based profes-sional development plan; based on annual staff appraisals.

4 Action plan for developing clinical governance

- Use the chart on page 24 to show how you are addressing clinical governance with several timetabled action programmes. Photocopy the three pages of the chart for separate exercises addressing different topics. Involve as many people in the practice as you can – it will share the burden of the work and gain ownership of the programme.

Your primary care group or primary care trust or other NHS trust

Keep up to date with the requirements for you to demonstrate the clinical governance culture that is developing across your PCG/PCT or trust.[8,9]

The four key steps are:

1 Establish leadership, accountability and working arrangements.
2 Carry out a baseline assessment of capacity and capability.
3 Formulate and agree a development plan in the light of this assessment.
4 Clarify reporting arrangements for clinical governance within board and annual reports.

Details of how to undertake a baseline review and implement a clinical governance pro-gramme across the PCG/PCT or trust from the board's strategic perspective are given else-where and are outside the scope of this book, which is aimed at grassroots practitioners.[9]

In brief, the evidence you will need to present to the board will include details of:

- your overall approach to clinical governance
- human resources, education, training and development, and appraisal initiatives to support clinical governance
- 'knowledge management', data and information systems to support clinical govern-ance – this will include such issues as confidentiality, record keeping, access to information
- **audit, evidence-based practice, and research and development initiatives to support clinical governance**
- complaints, risk management and adverse incident initiatives to support clinical governance
- your annual report describing your priorities for development – and justifying them by various means including public consultation.

Include information about your achievements and the opportunities of which you are aware for further development. Note your weaknesses too and describe how you are planning to overcome them.

PART TWO

The 14 themes of clinical governance

For each module:

- Key information about the topic
- Who could do what
- Your action plan
- Your evaluation plan
- Your record of learning

MODULE 1

Establishing and sustaining a learning culture

'Clinical indicators should be used to learn, not to judge.'[10] The fact that this needs stating shows how fragile the learning culture of the NHS really is. Medical students were traditionally humiliated if unable to come up with the right answer, in front of other students, patients and nursing staff. Clinical audit has sometimes been used to identify and expose people's shortcomings rather than provide opportunities for learning and improvement. League tables of performance have been used out of context, concealing that like was not necessarily being compared with like.

Clinical governance will only achieve health gains and improvements in the quality of healthcare if staff are not penalised for admitting mistakes and calling for more resources. Such a culture would help professionals and managers to work together to achieve the standards set out in the NSFs without apportioning blame for any shortfalls in service provision.

Topics covered in this module

- Establishing a learning culture that underpins clinical governance
- Education and training needs for *The New NHS*
- Learning to work in partnerships
- Drawing up educational programmes for your practice, PCG/PCT or NHS trust
- Making your own personal learning plan
- Appropriate mode of delivery
- Multiprofessional education
- Continuing professional development and lifelong learning
- Evidence-based education
- Proforma for assessing whether topic of learning is a priority

Establishing a learning culture that underpins clinical governance

An environment in which clinical effectiveness can flourish requires managers, clinicians and non-clinical support staff to work together with patients and the public.

The application of clinical governance in practice will require a learning culture that encourages:

- a sustained quality improvement culture
- motivated staff
- evaluation of changes in practice.

The components of clinical governance are already established concepts whose roots are based in a learning culture:

- high standards – of care and service provision
- reflective practice – learning from experience
- risk management – of clinical and organisational matters
- personal and team development.

As clinical governance is about delivering uniformly good care as a coordinated team, the basis of the learning environment is about staff learning together as a team. This applies whether the team works in a small unit, such as a single-handed general practice, or a much larger team, such as in a trust where different disciplines may work as subteams within the whole. The education and training plan for the team should address service and individuals' development; the strategy should focus on ways of implementing the education and development plan and overcoming barriers to its application.

Blocks and barriers[11] to establishing a coherent education and training programme across a practice, PCG or PCT include:

- isolation of health professionals, even many of those who appear to work in a team
- 'tribalism' as different disciplines protect their traditional roles and responsibilities
- lack of incentives to take up learner-centred, interactive education as opposed to more passive modes of educational delivery
- differing rights to time and funds for continuing education between staff in the same workplace
- lack of communication between health and social care organisations and individuals
- rigid educational budgets for different professionals
- practitioners overwhelmed with service work and with little time for continuing education
- dissonance between what individuals think they need to learn and what is relevant to service needs
- reluctance to develop or accept new models of working and extended roles

- mental ill health: depression, stress, burnout of learner or teacher
- fear of, and resistance to, change.

Education and training needs for *The New NHS*

There is sometimes confusion about the difference between 'education' and 'training'. Education and training can coexist. The two may be differentiated by thinking of:

- education as being about doing things better
- training as being about taking on new tasks.

Many in the NHS know little about how to commission and deliver healthcare that is better informed by local issues and targeted at local health needs. Evidence-based clinical care or health policy, or justifying performance where it diverts from best practice, are also common learning needs for many of the NHS workforce.

Such areas are complex and require as great an understanding of the context of healthcare as the topics themselves. For instance, learning more about 'health needs assessment' requires knowledge about the differences and inter-relationships between 'need' (the potential to benefit from care), 'demand' (expressed desire for services) and 'supply' (services that are actually provided in relation to need or demand), and will require NHS practitioners and managers to take a broader view of 'health' than just that which concerns individual patients.

New educational requirements of today's NHS

- Making education and training plans that complement the priorities of the practice, PCG/PCT or other NHS trust, district or central government
- The implementation of clinical governance: knowledge, positive attitudes, new skills and a learning culture
- Adoption of evidence-based practice and policy: where and how to get the information, how to apply the evidence and monitor changes
- Needs assessments: how to do them, who to work with, link with commissioning, ways to reduce health inequalities
- Working in partnerships with: other disciplines, clinicians and managers, clinicians and patients or the public, non-health organisations
- How best to involve the public and patients in decision making
- Understanding and working with new models of delivery of care
- Delivering tangible 'health gains' rather than improvements in structures and systems
- Encouraging a culture whereby research and development are inextricably linked

---

In a recent survey[12] of 512 primary health and social care professionals and managers, *health needs assessment* was the most consistently identified skill the majority of respondents thought that they needed; *clinical audit* and *strategic planning* were other skills most frequently cited.

Learning to work in partnerships

You can only learn about working in partnerships with others from various health disciplines, the voluntary sector or local authorities by doing it. Such learning is not gained from textbooks or lectures.

The traditional approach to education in the NHS has been to segregate the professions. This is no longer tenable. Service changes affect everyone and a coordinated approach will be needed at the local level if the health service is to deliver new models of care that are better targeted at the needs of the community.

Applying patient and public participation in decision making requires a change of attitudes and beliefs and not just an updating of knowledge and skills. To succeed in this, traditional boundaries such as those between clinicians and patients, or the NHS and voluntary sector will need to be broken down.

Employment terms and conditions in general medical practices and trusts are variable (*see* Module 2 Managing resources and services). Some, but not all, employees are granted study leave and financial support for course fees. Independent contractors (GPs, dentists, optometrists and pharmacists) may be limited by having to employ locums to allow their attendance at external courses or educational activities.

Preliminary work[13] establishing the education and training needs of GPs and community nurses in the Oxford region found that respondents wanted to learn more about team-working, planning and management, and public health skills. Networking between PCGs/PCTs and other NHS trusts should be important in sharing 'ideas, experiences and functions'.

Effective implementation of clinical governance will require working partnerships between:

- managers and clinicians in PCGs/PCTs, other NHS trusts and general practices
- those in acute, community and primary care sectors
- different disciplines in primary care
- health and social care services
- clinicians and users, carers and the general public
- NHS managers and users, carers and the general public
- information, quality, education, research, communication specialties
- champions or innovators and grassroots practitioners.

Drawing up educational programmes for your practice, PCG/PCT or NHS trust

Work-based learning includes:

- learning *for* work
- learning *at* work
- learning *from* work.[14]

The themes emerging to drive education and training in PCGs and trusts are about developing a better understanding of:

- the nature and implementation of NHS changes for all staff
- the organisation and funding of health-related education and workforce planning
- practical links between educational providers and PCGs /PCTs or other NHS trusts to support staff
- the educational and development needs of PCGs/PCTs and other NHS trusts
- the development of a population focus in PCGs/PCTs by clinicians and managers
- access and use of information to support learning.

General practices and directorates of trusts will have similar organisational needs. Appoint a lead person supported by a steering group in which the main disciplines are represented. Link with and cascade the strategy and plan to the grassroots.

Individuals' own educational plans should complement and dovetail into the overall business and development plans of their PCG or trust. These should incorporate central and district priorities as well as their own justified personal and professional development priorities.

Continuing education and development plans in practice

In a telephone survey of 100 general practices in 1999, 73% of responding practices had continuing education and development plans for practice staff; 27% had assessed staff training needs in the previous 12 months. Education and training needs were not identified by risk management or audit. Neither practice development activities nor district wide education for GPs were directed at local population health needs or priorities.[15]

Making your personal development plan

Your plan should encompass the context and culture of your working environment as well as the knowledge and skills relating to your post. Your personal learning plan might form the major part of a future professional revalidation programme. Your plan should:

- identify your weaknesses in knowledge, skills or attitudes
- specify topics for learning as a result of changes: in your role, responsibilities, the organisation
- describe how you identified your learning needs
- prioritise and set your learning needs and associated goals
- justify your selection of learning goals
- describe how you will achieve your goals and over what time period
- describe how you will evaluate learning outcomes.

Appropriate mode of delivery

People choose to learn in ways that they are used to, or are most convenient rather than the most appropriate for the topic they need to learn about

A recent survey of education and training needs showed how health professionals and managers opted for the mode of training with which they were most familiar (usually a lecture or validated professional course) or which suited their working conditions (for example distance learning for those who found it difficult to take study leave from their workplace, as pharmacists do). Few matched their educational requirements with the mode of delivery that was most appropriate for the topic.[12]

Lectures are only useful for transferring knowledge. If active discussion is an essential part of learning then you would be better joining in small group work and interactive discussion. Most of the new requirements of learning for the NHS require a change of attitudes and deeper understanding of others' views or experiences – difficult concepts to transmit via lectures.

Problem solving and thinking is an effective approach to learning. The seven stages are:[16]

1 Clarify terms and concepts in the problem.
2 Define the problem – set out what needs to be understood.
3 Analyse the problem – generate possible explanations.
4 Make a systematic inventory of the explanations – link ideas.
5 Formulate learning questions – what you need to be able to understand.
6 Collect information – try to find the answers.
7 Synthesise and test the information – test your answers and discuss the findings.

Learning about such complex subjects as clinical governance or teamworking involves:

- cultural change
- flexibility to adapt to new roles and responsibilities
- negotiation and political awareness.

Effective implementation of clinical governance will only be possible if the whole organisation is flexible to change in response to individuals' learning.

Education about the meaning of clinical governance could be delivered by a combination of paper-based activities, electronic newsletters, workshops, lectures, seminars and tutorials. Any such activities should be as interactive as possible to encourage a deeper understanding of the issues and the consequences of action or omission. People learn in different ways, so there should be a variety of methods of education and training on offer so that individuals can opt for the methods they prefer, by which they are more readily engaged and learn best.

Multiprofessional education

Multiprofessional education and training for the NHS workforce is envisaged as being integral to delivering the programme of modernisation of the NHS.[17]

There will always be a place for uniprofessional education. Some clinical or organisational subjects are so specialised that they only apply to one particular discipline or subspecialty of doctors, nurses or therapists. And there will be situations where one discipline is not confident learning alongside others from traditionally more dominant disciplines, or where the extent of their learning needs is very different.

Benefits of multiprofessional working and learning may be facilitating:[18,19]

- reduced isolation of professionals from different disciplines
- collaboration in meeting the needs of local communities
- increased understanding of others' roles and responsibilities
- opportunities to develop a more appropriate skill-mix of healthcare professionals
- the development of new roles
- professionals working together in an atmosphere of openness and trust
- real communication between professionals
- an appreciation of the strengths of the diversity of other professionals
- respect for others' professional judgement
- a common set of values and attitudes

Perceived barriers to multiprofessional shared learning are:[20]

- a lack of time – often used by doctors as an excuse for not attending in-house training
- the medical model inhibiting 'multiperspective communication'
- organisational structures and processes – making collaborative practice difficult to maintain
- mistaken assumptions about the meaning of multiprofessional learning being about topics that are common to everyone, rather than being about the different professions contributing to a coordinated team.

▼

Continuing professional development and lifelong learning

Continuing professional development has been defined as 'a process of lifelong learning for all individuals and teams which enables professionals to expand and fulfil their potential and ... meets the needs of patients and delivers the health and health care priorities of the NHS'.[21]

The principles of CPD apply to non-clinical staff just as much as clinicians. CPD includes: pursuing personal and professional growth through widening, developing and changing your own roles and responsibilities; keeping abreast of and accommodating clinical, organisational and social changes that affect professional roles in general; acquiring and refining the skills needed for new roles or responsibilities or career development; putting individual development and learning needs into a team and multiprofessional context.[22]

Criteria for successful learning[18]

The most successful continuing professional development involves learning which:

- is based on what is already familiar to the learner
- is led by the learner's own identified needs
- is problem-centred
- involves active participation by the learner
- uses the learner's own resources – built on their previous experiences
- includes relevant and timely feedback
- is given when the learner experiences the need to know something
- includes self-assessment.

Lifelong learning combines formal and informal learning as a natural part of everyone's everyday lives. Strong links between theory (the teaching), practice and health policy should ensure that lifelong learning applied to the NHS is relevant to service needs.

Evidence-based education (*see* Module 5 Evidence-based practice and policy)

Evidence-based education is as important as evidence-based health policy, practice or management. Teachers should regularly update their material by searching published literature from electronic databases such as the Cochrane Library, Medline or Cinahl. Health professionals have limited time for searching the literature, but providing the 'search strategy' is carefully planned, it should take only a few minutes to identify important publications.

A good search strategy[23] will have a well-framed question relating to the purpose of the enquiry. Key words should be chosen specifically to reflect the dimensions of the question to use with appropriate databases. Obtain and read complete papers rather than relying on interesting looking abstracts; then make up your own mind as to the reliability of the evidence applied to your own situation.

> The journal *Medical Teacher* has a useful series giving the 'best evidence in medical education' with expert opinion and interpretation backed by research evidence.

You could apply evidence-based education in your workplace tomorrow in teaching patients or junior colleagues. Start with a direct request from a patient for information on a health-related topic which they know little about. The evidence shows that the best way to help them learn is to:

- engage them so that they see learning as relevant and apply the information to themselves in their own situation
- understand where they are starting from; correct misconceptions and fill in gaps
- be aware that previous beliefs and competing pressures may constrain their acceptance of your new information
- activate previous knowledge
- limit the amount of new information.

Proforma for assessing whether topic of learning is a priority

Check out whether the topic you choose to learn is a priority and the way in which you plan to learn about it is appropriate. Photocopy this proforma for future use.

Your topic:

How have you identified your learning need(s)?

a	PCG requirement	❏	e	Appraisal need	❏
b	Practice business plan	❏	f	New to post	❏
c	Legal mandatory requirement	❏	g	Individual decision	❏
d	Job requirement	❏	h	Patient feedback	❏
			i	Other	❏

....

Have you discussed or planned your learning needs with anyone else?

Yes ❏   No ❏   If so, who? ....

What are the learning need(s) and/or objective(s) in terms of:

Knowledge: What new information do you hope to gain to help you do this?

....

Skills: What should you be able to do differently as a result of undertaking this development?

....

Behaviour/professional practice: How will this impact on the way you then do things?

....

Details and date of desired development activity:

....

Details of any previous training and/or experience you have in this area/dates:

....

Your current performance in this area against the requirements of your job:

Need significant development in this area ❏   Need some development in this area ❏
Satisfactory in this area ❏   Do well in this area ❏

Level of job relevance this area has to your role and responsibilities:

Has no relevance to job ❏   Has some relevance ❏
Relevant to job ❏   Very relevant ❏
Essential to job ❏

Describe what aspect of your job and how the proposed education/training is relevant:

....

Additional support in identifying a suitable development activity?

Yes ❏   No ❏

What do you need?

Describe the differences or improvements for you, your practice, PCG and/or trust as a result of undertaking this activity?

....

Determine the priority of your proposed educational/training activity:

Urgent ❏   High ❏   Medium ❏   Low ❏

Describe how the proposed activity will meet your learning needs rather than any other type of course or training on the topic:

....

If you had a free choice would you want to learn this? Yes/No

If **no**, why not? (please circle all that apply):

waste of time
already done it
not relevant to my work, career goals
other

If **yes**, what reasons are most important to you (put in rank order):

improve my performance
increase my knowledge
get promotion
just interested
be better than my colleagues
do a more interesting job
be more confident
it will help me

Some ideas on who should do what to establish a learning culture in your practice

The GP

- Give a lead on the importance of education for all staff.
- Take responsibility for good employer practices for your team.
- Provide adequate resources for all staff to have sufficient opportunities for learning and development.
- Draw up, carry out and evaluate your own professional development plan.

The practice manager

- Organise and review the practice-based professional development plan.
- Obtain facts and figures, subjective and objective data about learning needs to inform the practice-based plan.
- Encourage individuals to formulate and implement professional development plans.
- Encourage attached staff and independent contractors to be included in practice-based team learning.
- Undertake job appraisals for all staff; clarify learning needs and plan to address those needs.

- Identify suitable educational events and activities for staff.
- Recognise staff learning needs associated with clinical governance.

The practice nurse

- Draw up, carry out and evaluate own professional development plan.
- Contribute to teaching patients and colleagues about areas of your own expertise.
- Learn more about applying clinical governance in practice.

The receptionist

- Draw up, carry out and evaluate own professional development plan.
- Arrange and organise in-house educational meetings as requested.
- Help practice manager obtain baseline data about performance to inform practice-based plan and clinical governance programme.
- Pass on suggestions and comments from patients to practice manager that might serve to identify learning needs of the practice team.

Other attached staff: district nurse, health visitor, community psychiatric nurse, the therapist

- Draw up, carry out and evaluate own professional development plan.
- Contribute to practice-based professional development plan as team member and expert in your own specialty.
- Feed in ideas that help shape the clinical governance programme.

Action plan: learning culture

Today's date: ....

Action plan to be completed by: ....

Tackled by	Identify need/assess problem	Plan of action: what will you do?/by when?
Individual – you		
Practice team – you and your colleagues		
Organisation – your practice		

Evaluation: learning culture

Complete as evaluation of progress by ....

Level of evaluation: perspective or work done on this component by	The need or problem	Outcome: what have you achieved?	Who was involved in doing it?	Evaluated: • by whom? • when? • what method was used?
Individual – you				
Practice team – you and your colleagues				
Organisation – your practice				

Record of your learning about 'learning culture'

Write in topic, date, time spent, type of learning

	Activity 1	Activity 2	Activity 3	Activity 4
In-house formal learning				
External courses				
Informal and personal				
Qualifications and/or experience gained				

MODULE 2

Managing resources and services

Involves two overlapping categories:

PEOPLE and THINGS.

If you get the people right the organisation will have an excellent basis.

Topics covered in this module

- Getting the right person for the job
- Motivating people to do a better job
- Working in teams
- Dealing with change
- Education and training needs for the new NHS (*see* p. 35)
- Setting targets
- When things go wrong
- Endings and termination of employment
- Budgets
- Process management

You must also make sure that the things you need are in the right place at the right time and working correctly.

Getting the right person for the job
The job description

The clearer you are about what you need, the more likely you are to recruit well. Draft a job description that describes all the tasks and responsibilities of the position, together with the minimum qualifications and experience. If you are filling an existing position, ask the outgoing person to record all the things that are involved and review the list. Now is the time to add or remove any duties or requirements.

Now that the appointments were listed on the computer, the need for individual appointment lists for each consultation room had disappeared. The outgoing clerk had continued to print out a list and add hand-written alterations. When a new clerk was to be appointed, everyone was asked and all said they did not use the printed lists, so they were removed from the job description.

Where do you look?

Word of mouth is still the best method of recruitment. Your present workers know what is involved and they know the person to whom they are talking. They can often match the person to the job.

Internal recruitment means the individual is already known and knows the ethos of the organisation. Training someone whose skills, knowledge and attitudes you already know about may be a more certain way to get what you want than hoping to find the right person from within another organisation.

Temporary employment is a good way of trying people out before you employ them long term. Agency staff are particularly useful when you need someone urgently or are not sure for how long someone will be needed. They can try you out as well and can be consulted about the job description if they do not want the permanent job themselves.

Professional or workers associations often have advertising columns so that you can target your job opening. It is worth thinking about who will read your advertisement – you don't advertise for a computer whizz in the *Times Educational* supplement; an Internet site would be a better bet.

The interview

Use the job description to draw up an interview outline. You need to use this to make sure you check all the attributes and skills that you require *and* to show that you did not reject anyone because of bias or prejudice. Draft the questions beforehand, make them relevant to the job description and record all the answers to the questions. Take lots of notes or you will not remember who was who.

You need to ask people:

- why they have applied
- what they can do for your organisation

- how they would fit in with the present team of workers
- when they could start
- whether they will come for the money you can afford.

Make sure you let people know when they can expect an answer to their application. Ensure that your applicant confirms acceptance before notifying the others that they have not succeeded. *Always* check references before offering a job.

> Mrs H seemed ideal for the job, enthusiatic and charming. They were short-staffed. She was free to start immediately, so she was appointed, fortunately subject to satisfactory references. The manager rang the referees as none had been received. One merely said that she was not prepared to give a reference, the other exploded into anger over Mrs H's behaviour. Mrs H had left without giving notice when called for an official warning. The manager had an unpleasant interview with Mrs H to withdraw the offer of employment.

View references with caution; you may receive a good one because someone is glad the person is moving on, but has no firm evidence on which to condemn him or her.

Your candidates can be divided into those who:

- could do the job
- could do the job with extra training
- are not suitable.

Make sure you are not rejecting the last group because of their ethnic origin, sex, age, marital status, religion or disability (not only is this illegal, but may also prevent you getting the best person for the job).

Before the new employee starts

Plan how your new employee will know what to do. He/she needs a period to learn the ropes, preferably guided by someone who knows how to do the jobs listed in the job description. You will not get the best out of someone who has to find out everything from scratch. A new employee needs a mentor or a list of useful people to ask.

Employment law

You need to show that you are managing your staff correctly, so make sure that you provide:

- an up-to-date job description
- the terms of employment

- mutual assessment appraisals and individual training and development plans
- training in-house with other staff
- regular meetings with other staff and clear methods of communicating with them at other times
- knowledge of disciplinary and grievance procedures
- personnel records kept securely with access only to authorised people.

Motivating people to do a better job

Human nature makes people respond better to praise than punishment (if you need to do the latter see the sections below on 'When things go wrong' and 'Endings').

You cannot praise people unless you know what they are meant to be doing – so be aware of their goals and tasks. But you need to be careful not to become caught up in the details of how they achieve their goals or they will think that you do not trust them to do the job or that you have not made the transition from worker to manager.

It seems simple to decide to reward everyone equally – but is this motivating?

> Mr A completes a job before the time allocated for it and without any errors. Mr B runs over the time and the work contains several errors. You give Mr A some more work to do while Mr B struggles to complete his correctly. If you reward Mr A and Mr B equally, Mr A will feel punished and not at all motivated to do so well next time – all he gets is more work!

The best way to discover what motivates people is to ask them. Some will want more money, others more time, some more flexibility in their work schedule, others to do new and more challenging jobs. Observe how each person responds to the rewards you can offer.

Start with the positive and start with the small things. Most of us are not making earth-shattering advances every day, but little achievements and completions. The praise should come:

- immediately after the successful completion of part or all of the task
- from someone who knows what the task involved (not a remote committee)
- from an understanding of what the task involved.

Incentives that work include:

- personal or written congratulations from a respected colleague or immediate superior
- public recognition
- announcement of success at team meetings
- recognising that the last job was well done and asking for an opinion of the next one
- providing specific and frequent feedback (positive first)

- providing information on how the task has affected the performance of the organisation or management of a patient
- encouragement to increase their knowledge and skills to do even better
- making time to listen to ideas, complaints or difficulties
- learning from mistakes and making visible changes.

Working in teams

See Module 8 Coherent teamwork for a more detailed discussion of the development and evaluation of teams.

Clinical governance requires teamworking at all levels of the organisation with multi-professional consultation, education and training. Managers need to give effective leadership as well as enabling the correct mix of team members. Managers create the culture for change and usually control the resources through which change can occur.

A team may be clinical – in a trust or practice. Health professionals have to work together and with the patients. It may be organisational – an NHS trust or PCG/PCT – to support education and training to improve behaviour and attitudes, as well as managing audit, procedures, monitoring and risk.

Team members need to respect the skills and contributions of the other members of the team. All members should be clear about their roles and their responsibilities. Remember that each team member brings their worries and previous experience to meetings – look out for the hidden agendas beneath the table.

Clinical teams

Integrated nursing teams have existed for years but interdisciplinary teams require more development.[24] In a clinical team where members may have overlapping clinical responsibilities, make clear and unambiguous handover arrangements. Give the information necessary for good care, but remember the guidance on confidentiality (*see* Module 6 Confidentiality), especially if the patient does not want particular information shared with others.

Project teams

In a project team, consider the wider multidisciplinary aspects to your project. Some people find networking and building relationships with other staff difficult.

Consider:

- who leads a multidisciplinary group?
- how do you find out who to contact?

- how do you reconcile different priorities and perspectives?
- what is your contribution to any difficulties working with other people?

Time away from the workplace to reflect with a tutor or coach, or discussion with colleagues who are not involved, can help to resolve difficulties and provide fresh insights.

A problem of poor direction signs is identified in an elderly care hospital. A project team is set up. The project team of administrative and clinical workers suggested consulting:

- the existing literature on signs in health service and architectural journals and documents
- users – patients, relatives, friends, staff
- the Health and Safety Officer
- management for availability of resources and making any changes happen and expanding the multidisciplinary nature of the team.

Clinical improvement teams

Include nurses, doctors, paramedics, pharmacists, therapists, and other operational staff and clinical leads in clinical improvement teams. Consider how best to involve the public in your decisions.[25]

A key area is to specify precisely what is provided. Individual patient care involves a selection of services to provide diagnosis, assessment and/or treatment. Each patient differs from another so service units group patients into broadly similar cases (case-mix). The basis for classifying patients into groups depends on why you need the information.

Accurate coding of patient illness is needed (*see* Module 4 Reliable and accurate data). Patients within the same diagnostic group are likely to require equivalent complexity of care. However, if you are looking at very different age groups with the same diagnosis you may need a more sophisticated case-mix.[26]

Case-mix management is usually carried out by computer systems that bring together all the information by transfer of data from other operational systems. This requires suitable interfaces between systems and validation of the data to derive standard costs for each case-mix group (in the NHS they are called Healthcare Resource Groups, HRGs; HRGs are being developed by the National Case Mix Office, 1 St Cross Road, Winchester SO23 9AJ). Beware of making changes to systems based on inaccurate or incomplete data. Always look at whether the information seems reasonable and whether there are large variations from expected profiles. Consider also the ethical implications. If a patient will cost more than the average for that case-mix is there a risk that the patient will be denied treatment?

The objectives for clinical improvement teams may include:

- identification of problem areas and making recommendations to the clinical lead
- assessment of clinical risk and implementing corrective action

- communication of potential risks to patients and staff
- examination of clinical incidents, claims or complaints and recommendation of remedial action
- consultation with the public about identifying service changes needed
- development of guidelines, standards, audit, procedures, care pathways, clinical policies and other actions to improve or change clinical practice
- identification of training needs and recommendations about implementation
- provision of a forum for open discussion of performance monitoring, problems and development.

Management teams and board members

Training helps managers and board members to understand:

- how best practice is identified
- how practice can be monitored
- how clinical staff function
- what clinical risk management means
- how complaints can be used to influence constructive change
- how they can review staff performance.

A partnership between clinical and administrative staff allows them to make constructive challenges and support each other in the development of quality.

Three dimensional co-ordination and management

Think about managing and coordinating in different directions – not only managing and relating to the staff who are responsible to you but in all directions (*see* Figure M2.1).

Figure M2.1   Three-dimensional coordination and management.

Dealing with change

Change happens all the time. Think how you can help to make transitions occur smoothly by:

- deciding on what needs to be changed through gathering evidence
- sharing the responsibility for identifying the problem and finding the solutions so that everyone feels part of the process (ownership)
- building in plenty of time to discuss the planned changes so that everyone feels that they have had a chance to put their point of view
- making the changes in small steps
- giving plenty of support and monitoring progress
- giving feedback so that everyone knows how the changes are progressing and what their part in them means to the whole
- celebrating completion and continuing monitoring to prevent backsliding.

Despite the excitement that changes can bring we tend to resist change. To improve quality, change is inevitable.

Recognise the signs of resistance in yourself and in others if you:

- use outdated methods
- avoid new duties or ways of working
- control and resist the change
- play the victim and use others to do the new work
- wait for someone else to implement it
- stop being able to do your present work properly.

Try going on a course to learn how to do the new task, ask for support from other people, take some time out to do something different, develop other interests ... or change jobs!

Is some of your information *still* on a card index or in an index book?

Think about four levels of change:

- Do we need to do something new?
- Should we do things differently – change a system or process?
- Should we do something different – change the purpose?
- Do we need to stop doing something – does the service or organisation need to exist at all?

Organisations are like weather systems, constantly changing and shifting. If you change one thing here, it affects many others. The environment constantly alters so the outside influences need constant monitoring. Strategies have to be flexible. People have to be supported in coping with the constant change. Remember to involve them from the outset and keep them informed and part of the change process. Give time to grieve for the past and time for criticism and interchange of ideas. Imposing change breeds resentment and resistance.

* What makes *you* want to change?
* What are *your* barriers to change?

Setting targets

People react better if they have a direction of travel. Wandering around aimlessly makes you frustrated and disappointed.

Look at the self-assessment rating charts at the end of each module and think how you can use them for improving quality in a particular area. A SWOT (strengths, weaknesses, opportunities and threats) analysis[27] helps you to plan (*see* Chapter 2 on identifying learning needs). You need to identify what needs doing, whether it can be done, how it can be done, who needs to be involved, by when it needs to be done and how you will know when it is complete.

Remember to KISS (keep it simple and short), and pick two or three targets to focus on. If you set up too many targets you will not finish any and everyone will become discouraged.

There is an excellent poster that says:

FOR EVERY PROBLEM
THERE IS A SIMPLE SOLUTION AND IT'S
WRONG

Simple problems have a simple solution: Problem A ——————▶ Solution A. Most problems in resources and services are highly complex:

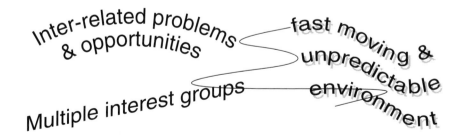

Figure M2.2 Problems in resources and services.

The so-called 'wicked problems' in *Helping Doctors Who Manage*[28] are describing problems that are complex, with interrelated parts, so that what seems like a solution for one part has bad effects on other parts and creates new problems elsewhere. The constantly changing environment changes the problems, so that any plans made become almost instantly out of date or the consequences unpredictable. Many people have an interest in the target solution and will all have different opinions, biases and priorities. You cannot please them all. In the NHS, an added dimension is the human lives and suffering of the individuals. Plans cannot be made in isolation from the effects that they have on healthcare for patients. Staff see the patients as individuals and each one as a priority for resources and services.

When things go wrong

Human beings are, well, human, and they make mistakes. They also vary a lot and may have poor attitudes. Part of clinical governance is making individuals accountable for setting, maintaining and monitoring performance standards.

To improve quality assurance use a stepwise approach as in the table below.

Table M2.1   Steps to improve quality assurance

Step	Action	Result
1	Use clear quality standards	90% of patients should be seen within 15 minutes of their appointment time
2	Monitor to compare performance with standards	A weekly audit graph is produced
3	Draw clear lines of managerial authority to take action if performance does not match standards	The appointments manager discusses the problem with the appointment clerks and with the clinicians to correct any problems
4	Be clear about the difference between advisory and management functions	The practice team discusses the frequency of recall for chronic conditions and advises. The appointments manager arranges for clinical staff to give timings of common procedures to the patients to book for the correct length of time
5	Encourage performance management by having clear accountability at each level with information passing from one level to another as appropriate	Staff members monitor their own timekeeping and pass information to the appointments manager so that a predictable late arrival on one day does not cause unwarranted delay

Dealing with poor performance requires better self-regulation (coming under the new accreditation systems), better systems of mentoring and supervision, the use of continuous professional education certification and whistle-blowing responsibility for all without recriminations (*see* the section on implementation in Module 5 Evidence-based practice and policy for ideas on how to assess performance).

The steps for dealing with unacceptable performance include:

- verbal discussion and plans for training or change linked to remedies for the documented and specific deficiency, i.e. evidence-based procedures
- written counselling and plans for training or change
- warnings about poor performance or attitudes
- job reallocation to more supervised tasks or demotion to lesser responsibility
- termination of employment.

Endings and termination of employment

See section on 'When things go wrong' above for what to do before you get to this stage.

Resignation

Sometimes people leave voluntarily. If you do not know why they left find out before the reasons affect their successors. Put a plan into place to make changes to avoid the same thing happening.

> Two nurses left in quick succession to take up jobs in adjacent areas. An enquiry into the reasons found an autocratic system of team management that they had found oppressive. No reporting system where these complaints could be heard had been established, so they left.

You may encourage resignation or early retirement when the rectifying or disciplinary actions taken have had insufficient effect and no alternative can be found.

> Dr B has become increasingly nervous of making mistakes as he ages. He brings patients back for review too often and orders unnecessary tests. He found that attending post-graduate education events made him even more nervous of doing the wrong thing and has decided to take earlier retirement than he originally planned.

Involuntary retirements

Redundancies do occur even in the understaffed NHS. Make sure that you follow the correct legal procedures. Termination of employment for serious offences is fortunately rare. Ensure you follow the correct legal framework. Offences meriting dismissal include:

- breaches of confidence
- violence or abuse
- misuse of drugs
- failure to carry out responsibilities or duties
- theft or fraud
- malpractice.

Timing of terminations of employment

Consider the feelings of the person who is leaving and time the leaving to cause the minimum of embarrassment. Give them time to clear out their belongings and say farewell. Not only does this minimise resentment but also gives remaining staff the feeling that they are being treated as human beings not automatons.

Budgets

Organisations have to make hard decisions about how to get value for money.[27,29] Whenever a different service, treatment or technology appears find out:

- how effective it is
- if it is cost-effective: whether an existing or rival technology is slightly less effective but cheaper and would be better used as a first choice
- whether investing in that technology will cause harm elsewhere because of a limited budget: will we need to cut services in order to introduce it?
- how it will affect the way the organisation is run
- what other resources will be needed to support it
- how much of it will be needed.

Budgets you need include:

- staff
- the purchase of equipment, etc. (capital expenditure)
- the purchase of drugs, appliances, stationery, etc. (consumables)
- maintenance and insurance.

Base your budgetary decision making on budgets on the items in the section on implementation in Module 5 Evidence-based practice and policy.

Further reading

There are quite a few books out there with varying styles and emphases. They tend to reflect the personal experiences of the authors or are selective in the aspects they describe. They may or may not suit your style of practice. Dip into them first from the library before investing your money – some of them are quite expensive.

- Bolden KJ *et al.* (1992) *Practice Management.* Blackwell Science, Oxford.
- Chartered Institute of Management Accountants Working Party (1992) *Financial Management within GP Practices.* Chartered Institute of Management Accountants, London.
- Forster HR (1995) *Practice Management Handbook.* BMJ Publishing Group, London.
- Fry J (1990) *Practice Management Compendium.* Kluwer Academic Publishers, Dordretch.
- Jones RVH *et al.* (1985) *Running a Practice: manual of practice management.* Chapman & Hall, London.
- Kehoe S (ed) (1999) *Primary Healthcare Premises.* Radcliffe Medical Press, Oxford.
- Patterson HR (1998) *Tutorials in Management in General Practice.* Churchill Livingstone, London.
- Vetter N (1999) *Clinically Effective Purchasing: a guide for primary care organisations.* Radcliffe Medical Press, Oxford.

Process management

Computerisation is increasingly important in monitoring what is happening to people and things in your organisation.[30] Maintaining services includes managing:

Who is where?	To locate staff and patients as they move about your facilities or sites or to keep a record of all encounters
What is where?	Track the records, the patients' samples, the equipment, etc., to ensure that you can get at it when you need it, i.e. accessibility is maximised and losses are minimised
Do we have enough?	Stock control – so that you do not run out
When do we need some more?	Track inward and outward movements to predict reordering times
When does it need servicing or replacing?	Have a regular routine for this to prevent sudden failure or unexpected expenditure
Who is responsible?	The buck stops there!

Delegation

One person does not have to do all of this. Each person should be responsible for his or her sphere of activity. Just as you know what is in the drawers of your desk (do you?), the practice nurse should know what is in her cupboards or stock room and the receptionist should know about the records. Sometimes simple methods are best.

> The practice manager was increasingly frustrated by complaints from the nurses that equipment disappeared from the treatment rooms. It sometimes reappeared several days later or was found in another room. Recording showed that a significant amount of time was wasted searching for it. After a multidisciplinary meeting a procedure was agreed. A book recording the equipment was kept in each treatment room. Each time someone borrowed it they were expected to write down their name and where it was being taken. When returned the entry was crossed out. Although the recording system was not always followed, only a few items were not returned. The system was shown to reduce the time wasted searching for missing equipment.

Some ideas on who should do what to manage resources and services in your practice

The GP

- Be clear about what tasks and responsibilities are delegated to the practice manager.
- Demonstrate your commitment to teamwork.
- Offer real support to your practice manager in his or her role.
- Make sure you recruit the right practice manager for your particular practice.

The practice manager

- Set up clear lines of accountability for all tasks and responsibilities that are delegated to staff.
- Keep good records about staffing matters, resources and services.
- Be consistently good at managing change. Find ways to overcome other people's reluctance to conform to new situations.
- Know what good recruitment and employment practices are and apply them consistently.

The practice nurse

- Continually try to improve your clinical practice.
- Anticipate change.
- Work within your capability – don't agree to undertake tasks for which you are insufficiently trained.
- Organise the equipment in the consulting and treatment rooms so that it is safe.

The receptionist

- Support the practice manager in organising the practice on a day-to-day basis.
- Take pride in the practice.

Other attached staff: district nurse, health visitor, community psychiatric nurse, the therapist

- Keep to any codes of conduct in the practice.
- Be fair about using resources from your trust and the general practice to which you are attached.
- Try to fit in with any new models of working with the practice team.

Action plan: managing resources and services

Today's date: ....   Action plan to be completed by: ....

Tackled by	Identify need/assess problem	Plan of action: what will you do?/by when?
Individual – you		
Practice team – you and your colleagues		
Organisation – your practice		

Evaluation: managing resources and services

Complete as evaluation of progress by ....

Level of evaluation: perspective or work done on this component by	The need or problem	Outcome: what have you achieved?	Who was involved in doing it?	Evaluated: • by whom? • when? • what method was used?
Individual – you				
Practice team – you and your colleagues				
Organisation – your practice				

Record of your learning about 'managing resources and services'

Write in topic, date, time spent, type of learning

	Activity 1	Activity 2	Activity 3	Activity 4
In-house formal learning				
External courses				
Informal and personal				
Qualifications and/or experience gained				

MODULE 3

Establishing and disseminating a research and development culture

Developing a research and development culture in primary care should encourage the wider adoption of evidence-based practice by all practitioners. This in turn should lead to increasingly appropriate patient management and more cost-effective prescribing practices. The NSFs are based on the evidence we have of best practice (*see* Module 5 Evidence-based practice and policy).

But the gulf between academics and clinicians seems as wide as ever. Academics do not always convey their conclusions in ways that enable practitioners to make informed choices about treatment options. It is common for clinicians to criticise researchers for not studying patients in real-life situations, believing that some academics have lost touch with everyday patient care. The flaws in some research studies lead to a distrust of research results in general.

The Department of Health and the NHS spends nearly £500 million per annum on research; in addition, industry (mainly pharmaceuticals) spends about £2500 million, medical charities more than £400 million and the Medical Research Council nearly £300 million per annum. Little of this research funding is invested in primary care issues or settings. It is intended that future research and funding will be more in line with NHS priorities and needs, and the health of communities, and will encourage networks of research and development activity.

Topics covered in this module

- Research in primary care
- Establishing a research and development culture in your PCG or PCT
- Establishing a research and development culture in your practice
- Involving consumers in health research
- Critical appraisal
- Good practice with questionnaires in general
- A protocol for carrying out a patient survey using a self-completion questionnaire

---

Research in primary care

The 'NHS Research and Development strategy aims to create a knowledge based health service in which clinical, managerial and policy decisions are based on sound information about research findings and service developments'.[31]

Research and development are essential activities in the understanding of whether or not care is effective, and how to make best use of resources. But there is a considerable gap that needs to be bridged between research findings 'proving' best practice, and health professionals and managers applying those findings in their everyday work. The true benefits of research and development will only be realised when there is a demonstrable impact on patient care from practitioners implementing lessons from research as a routine aspect of their work.

Primary care practitioners often feel that research is someone else's priority and they may not recognise the real contribution they make from altering interventions in response to policy changes or newly acquired knowledge.

A multidisciplinary approach to primary care research and development is important. Primary care is generally acknowledged to be a vastly under-researched area. Primary care research encompasses: epidemiology and the natural history of conditions; the clinical encounter; the patient perspective of care and engagement of the public in decision making; the organisation of the delivery of healthcare services; delivery of care across the interfaces of health, social care and local authority organisations; management of resources and implementing change.

Establishing a research and development culture in your PCG or PCT

Despite the gulf between academia and everyday practice, many clinicians harbour latent desires to do some research in a small way themselves. The research strategy in your PCG or PCT should harness this enthusiasm for scientific enquiry, while restraining clinicians from dashing off poorly thought-out studies that are not completed. Without expert academic support and guidance, novice researchers may soon be overwhelmed by service commitments and the enormity of what they have taken on. Such research may put patients needlessly at risk if novice practitioners are not aware of the dangers of their method or how intrusive their research is on patients. They may not realise that they should gain ethical approval of their research protocol before beginning the study.

Start by mapping out what expertise you have within your PCG or PCT in scientific methodology and who you might call on from outside your organisation. There will be experts in your local university, support from your NHS Executive regional office, and health professionals and managers who have completed higher research degrees. National organisations such as the Association of University Departments of General Practice (AUDGP) support members in undertaking scientific research. Some areas have networks of research practices linked to local universities, the Medical Research Council or national research and development Culyer funding.

You might set up a working group to coordinate the research effort in your PCG/PCT or district, as described in the box below.

Strengthening the research and development capability in North Staffordshire

The health authority has pulled together key people with a special interest or expertise in research from local universities, trusts, health promotion, practices and practitioners. They aim to strengthen the local capability. The plan includes:

- mapping research capabilities of trusts, local universities, practices and practitioners
- identifying priority areas for local research and development
- promoting research areas where local expertise/strength exists
- promoting an 'R & D' culture among the NHS workforce
- facilitating the application of evidence-based practice
- addressing the gap between clinical behaviour and knowledge of best practice
- linking primary care research to trials of interventions in the field.

You will need to make a work programme for your PCG or PCT to take forward each section of your plan. You might run research skills courses for enthusiastic would-be researchers, and critical appraisal skills courses to enable health professionals and managers to have a greater understanding of the limitations of published research reports. Think of ways to narrow the gap between knowing the evidence for best practice and applying it; such as through workshops to draw up clinical care pathways.

Establishing a research and development culture in your practice

Unless you have an expert in your practice team or are already part of a research network you will be better focusing on 'development' rather than 'research'. Your approach will include:

- understanding how to find out more about the evidence for best practice in investigation, management or treatment in clinical practice or organisational matters
- knowing how to access the findings in published literature and research papers
- creating an infrastructure with access to the evidence – an up-to-date practice library, staff time to visit the local medical library, links to the Internet and appropriate databases, links to other sources of information about your practice population (public health, mortality and morbidity rates, housing, employment, etc.)
- links to the local university or college as appropriate to your particular areas of interest; think widely – it might be that a School of Engineering can offer you help and support in developing a novel practical device for patient care
- knowing of or arranging skills training on research methods: for instance, questionnaire surveys or focus groups – from your postgraduate centre or regional workshops
- collaborating with others with more expertise as a way of getting started; identify and enter suitable patients in their studies having obtained your patients' informed consent
- learning about project management, gaining funds, making applications for ethical approval
- holding a journal club in your practice to present and debate interesting and current published papers as a multidisciplinary group
- looking for topics that are important to your local community – could you investigate a particular health issue? Is a new model of delivery of care worth piloting?
- recording all contacts with patients in a more systematic way to enable you to undertake research on your practice population more readily
- encouraging the integration of evaluation in all aspects of practice work.

Don't bite off more than you can chew – keep any research work focused on the question and purpose of the study. Try to find protected time and funds to employ secretarial assistance. Remember to protect confidential information and to seek informed consent from any patients you invite to join a study (*see* Module 6 Confidentiality). Be honest with potential subjects about what the research will entail – particularly if there may be more intensive tests or interventions later on. Disseminate conclusions from your research to as wide an audience as possible.

Involving consumers in health research (*see* Module 10 Meaningful patient and public involvement)

The involvement of consumers in research can have an important influence on the type of research undertaken and the ways in which it is carried out and disseminated. The lay perspective at the planning stage reminds researchers about patients' priorities and keeps the research plan firmly focused on real-life situations.[32]

We need consumer involvement in research to:

- get a consumer perspective on health research – priorities, ethics of the way in which it is conducted
- get research on consumer views – to give feedback to practising clinicians and managers
- get a consumer perspective on the development of outcome measures – so that outcomes relating to patients' values or views are meaningful and important
- describe experiences of suffering ill health or receiving care
- make decisions about the implications and application of the results.

Critical appraisal

Reading and evaluating a paper is mainly about applying common sense. Critical appraisal is a basic skill that any health professional can readily learn and apply to his or her own situation. You will soon discover for yourself some of the common flaws in published studies, sometimes even those in respected peer-reviewed journals where mistakes were overlooked by the publication team.

In general you should consider whether:[23,33]

- the paper is relevant to your own practice and results generalisable to your own circumstances
- the research question is clear and well-defined
- any definitions are unambiguous
- the context of the study is described
- the aim(s) and/or objective(s) of the study are clearly stated
- the design and methodology are appropriate for the aim(s) and question posed
- the measuring instruments seem to be reliable so that different assessors at different points in time would make the same observations
- the investigator is actually measuring that which she/he intends to measure
- the sampling method is clear
- the outcomes chosen to evaluate any intervention are appropriate

- the results relate to the aim(s) and objective(s) of the study
- the results seem to be robust and justifiable
- there are any biases in the method or the results, such as non-reporting of drop-outs from the study
- any unanticipated outcomes are explained
- the conclusions are valid
- you have any other concerns about the study.

Good practice with questionnaires in general

Questionnaires are often used by first-time researchers as the tool of choice for finding out the answer to their research question. They may mistakenly believe that undertaking a questionnaire survey is one of the simplest and easiest methods. Unfortunately for them, designing and employing a questionnaire is full of pitfalls and it is one of the most difficult techniques to use to gain a true or valid answer to the question posed.

Questions in a valid questionnaire will:

- be relevant and appropriate to the purpose of the enquiry
- be unambiguous
- contain one idea or enquiry at a time
- have an easily answered format with simple choices of response
- flow in a logical order
- not make assumptions
- use appropriate language likely to be understood by all respondents
- not be biased or leading
- not be offensive.

For the results to be valid and accurate the respondents must be representative of the target population. The response rate should be high and as near to 100% as possible.

Pilot your draft questionnaire on people who will not be in your final survey. The pilot should detect problems with your questions or method.

Benefits of a postal questionnaire survey

- it is relatively cheap as it does not involve interviewers
- one skilled person can design the project; less-skilled staff undertake data collection
- repeatable
- can be distributed over a wide geographical area
- can obtain the views of many people, although a big survey is costly

Drawbacks of a postal questionnaire survey

- relatively time-consuming with chasing up non-respondents and carrying out analyses
- response rates tend to be lower than for interview surveys
- people who are illiterate, have learning disabilities, are visually impaired, suffer mental health problems, elderly people and those from ethnic minority groups with poor English language skills are unlikely to complete questionnaires
- cannot be sure who has answered it
- respondents may give dishonest answers
- respondents cannot clarify a question they do not fully understand
- people may give their opinion about topics they know nothing or little about

A protocol for carrying out a patient survey using a self-completion questionnaire

If you decide to undertake a survey of patients' views on an issue (*see* Module 10 Meaningful patient and public involvement), write out your protocol first so that you adopt a scientific design and do not make up the method as you go along.[25]

1 Decide the exact question being posed. Write down the purpose or aim of the survey.
2 Define your target population.
3 Consider the extent of resources available to undertake the survey – your and others' time, expertise in designing, coding and analysing, funds for printing and postage etc.
4 Write out the timetabled protocol – the number to be sampled, how sampling will be carried out, description of pilot phase, the method of delivery of the questionnaire, how completed questionnaires will be returned, how and when non-respondents will be chased up, the outcomes by which achievement of the purpose will be measured, dissemination of results, likely action plan resulting.
5 Find out if an established and valid questionnaire already exists, such as the *General Practice Assessment Survey*,[34] which measures access and availability, technical care, inter-personal care, continuity of care, trust, contextual knowledge,

practice nursing care, referral and coordination of care outside the practice. It is freely available to use. If no appropriate questionnaire exists, design your own. Carry out preliminary work gathering people's views as to the content and purpose of the survey.

6 Adopt the usual wording of your target population – keep the questionnaire reasonably short, don't include any unnecessary or meaningless questions.

7 Try out the questionnaire on people who will not be among your sampled population. Ask them to give you constructive feedback on your questions. Check that the coding frame works for the responses you receive. Refine your questionnaire and method accordingly.

8 Start your survey. Make it easy for respondents to return the questionnaires with stamped addressed envelopes, a freepost address, easily accessible collection boxes, etc.

9 Remind non-respondents once or twice, depending on your resources, time frame and how important it is to have as good a response rate as possible.

Some ideas on who should do what to establish a research and development culture in your practice

The GP

- Give a lead in establishing research and development in the practice; for instance make resources available or include the topic in your business and development plan.
- Cooperate with any research studies being undertaken in the practice by referring patients on to the researcher as appropriate.
- Apply evidence of best practice to your everyday clinical work.

The practice manager

- Find out where and when there are research skills training workshops.
- Map out expertise and resources for research and development in the practice.
- Apply evidence of best practice to your everyday management and policy making.

The practice nurse

- Cooperate with any research studies based in the practice.
- Apply evidence of best practice to your everyday clinical work.

The receptionist

- Help to collect data for any research studies undertaken in the practice.
- Help to monitor whether research studies are adversely affecting service work.

Other attached staff: district nurse, health visitor, community psychiatric nurse, the therapist

- Apply evidence of best practice to your everyday clinical work.

Action plan: research and development culture

Today's date: .... Action plan to be completed by: ....

Tackled by	Identify need/assess problem	Plan of action: what will you do?/by when?
Individual – you		
Practice team – you and your colleagues		
Organisation – your practice		

Evaluation: establishing a research and development culture

Complete as evaluation of progress by ....

Level of evaluation: perspective or work done on this component by	The need or problem	Outcome: what have you achieved?	Who was involved in doing it?	Evaluated: • by whom? • when? • what method was used?
Individual – you				
Practice team – you and your colleagues				
Organisation – your practice				

Record of your learning about 'establishing a research and development culture'

Write in topic, date, time spent, type of learning

	Activity 1	Activity 2	Activity 3	Activity 4
In-house formal learning				
External courses				
Informal and personal				
Qualifications and/or experience gained				

MODULE 4

Reliable and accurate data

Clinicians, patients and administrators need reliable and accurate data to connect individuals or their healthcare records to other knowledge that is relevant to the care of the patient.

The purpose of the 'Information for Health' strategy is to help patients receive the best care and enable health professionals to provide care and improve the health of the public. The strategy includes the topics listed in the box below.

Topics included in this module

- Using data effectively
- Lifelong electronic health records for everyone
- Secure access at all times to patient records
- Information about best practice for clinicians
- Fast and convenient public access to information and care through online information services and telemedicine
- The effective use of NHS resources by providing health planners and managers with the information they need
- Sharing of information between GPs, community services and hospitals to provide seamless care

---

Don't forget that data also needs to be confidential (*see* Module 6 Confidentiality).

Using data effectively

To use data effectively we need to connect all of the following information systems:

Clinical record systems	
Electronic guidelines and applications supporting decision making	Epidemiological and audit (*see* Module 9 Audit and evaluation)

Clinical outcome databases	
Patient and health professional education and information products	Quality assessment tools accessible to patients

General practice, hospital and community management of patient care	
Needs assessment (*see* Module 5 Evidence-based policy and practice)	Management of resources and services (*see* Module 2 Managing resources and services)

Everything connects with everything and all support each other.

Lifelong electronic health records (EHR) for everyone

Using computers to capture, organise and display information has many advantages. It avoids the duplication of data entry as illustrated by the example of Mr B.

Mr B has an ingrowing toenail. It frequently becomes infected and he takes time off work. The chiropody service has had their tender for this work accepted. Mr B sees his doctor, who writes a clinical note in the record (first record). He then dictates to the secretary (second record), who types it out and adds the patient identifier (third record). The appointments clerk enters the request (fourth record) and sends an appointment. When Mr B is seen and treated, the chiropodist makes a clinical record (fifth record) and writes a letter to the referring doctor (sixth record). The letter is added to the bulging file and cannot easily be found at a later date. The chiropodist makes an entry on a form to record the activity (seventh record) to make a claim for the work. The doctor records the activity on another form (eighth record) so that payment can be made.

The problems shown by this example are that:

- the basic data set of patient identifiers is entered many times over; time and effort are wasted
- the clinical data relating to one episode is not all available in one place, but has to be searched for – sometimes without result
- the opportunity for errors is multiplied each time an entry is made
- it is difficult, if not impossible, to keep accurate and useful records of activity and demand for management and accounting.

As for monitoring quality:

> Quality = 'doing the right thing at the right time for the right person in the right way, and doing it right first time'.

Electronic health records can:

- record the information once
- record the information accurately by using templates or on-screen prompts
- display the information in a variety of ways, such as a summary, an episode or a chronological account – or a stock list, a waiting list, a priority group for action
- make the information accessible to a variety of people, from clinicians to administrators and policy makers
- make each part of the information subject to different levels of access so that, for example, personal medical information is not available to the accounts clerk
- supplement information not easily available by other means, such as how long people wait when they attend for their appointment
- be consulted remotely across long distances.

The next illustration of Mr W shows what can be done as soon as the necessary equipment is available and data entry is completed. The technology is available to do it now.

Mr W is admitted to hospital in Glasgow in 2001 with severe abdominal pain and a urinary tract infection. He has several scars on the abdomen, is elderly and confused. His daughter does not know what operations he has had. His EHR in Bradford is accessed electronically. This shows that he has had several recent admissions for partial obstruction managed conservatively, following surgery for ulcerative colitis 15 years ago. The staff are helped by the record to decide against surgery. They do not give him penicillin-based antibiotic for the infection, as his record also alerts them that he is allergic to penicillin.

Secure access at all times to patient records

A paper record has inherent disadvantages:

- it cannot be in two places at once
- it is difficult to find the information you want in a mass of paper sheets
- it is inefficient – time is wasted looking for the record, looking in the record, copying out information that is in it
- it is bulky and difficult to store efficiently.

Make records easy to use so that you:

- minimise the training needed to use them
- prevent security procedures being circumvented
- record or retrieve information at the correct time
- reduce repetitive routine tasks
- enter or retrieve information in a standardised manner
- facilitate communication between all health staff
- incorporate audit and risk management
- base management and policy decisions on accurate information.

The Good European Health Record project was established to develop a common health record architecture, published in the public domain, for Europe.[35]

A useful article summarising the advantages of smart cards that have already been subject to trials has been published.[36] This future is available now for Mr T.

The physiotherapist Mr T arrives at the outreach clinic and inserts his personal code into the terminal on the desk. The machine starts up. The screen configures to his preferences and links to his level of access on the main screen. Miss L arrives at reception and gives in her personal number. The receptionist calls up her part of the record and confirms the details with the patient before sending her in. Mr T asks how Miss L is doing and updates the clinical record. The treatment is given and Miss L asks to be transferred to a clinic nearer home for the next treatment. This is agreed. Mr T knows that the record will be available to his colleague Mrs M at the other venue. The receptionist calls up the appointment list for the other clinic on to the screen and makes Miss L an appointment.

The manager of the physiotherapy department is looking at the numbers attending the clinics. Non-clinical information is collected automatically and she can see how many patients have been seen and what the waiting list is. She notes that the time patients are waiting to be seen in one clinic is twice as long as the average. She sends an email to the relevant staff member to ask for the reasons for this. He emails back with a list to show her that the case-mix is too heavy for the allocated time, so she adjusts the appointment times. The stock list for the appliances is maintained at each clinic and orders automatically from stores.

All it needs is the necessary investment and will to implement it!

Patient-held records are popular with patients. Smart cards can have different levels of access for different people. For example a pharmacist could access the medication record but not the results of someone's chest X-ray.

Information about best practice for clinicians

We all grumble about too much paperwork and cannot keep up with the reading that we ought to do. New data gathered in abstract is easily forgotten; what we need is accurate information accessible at the time that the problem presents.

Vast numbers of papers are published – 20 000 biomedical journals and 17 000 books every year. Much of the information is dubious. It is impossible for most people to weigh the evidence about every subject about which they need good-quality information.

Information technology can make some contributions:

- Search technology can retrieve abstracts of relevant publications.
- Libraries or user sites can keep you up to date with most of the published data on selected subjects using key words.
- Best evidence summaries produced by committees of reviewers are published[37] (*see* below for a useful list of Internet sites).

The National Electronic Library for Health should play an increasing role in the organisation, accreditation and updating of clinical reference material. It will be available on NHSnet – and the intention is to make this available from a terminal on every GP's desk. However, it is difficult to see how the time to consult it during working hours will be made available! Other health professionals and staff will not only have to find the time but also a suitable access point.

The following example shows how useful electronic access at the point of contact with the patient can be.

Mrs M attends with Darren. They are new patients to you and you have no previous notes. She tells you that Darren has Hurler's syndrome. You have never encountered this before and do not know the implications. You click on the Internet icon on your screen, and go to PubMed for access to Medline. This gives several recent articles, one of which gives an abstract containing the criteria for diagnosis and the implications. You are now in a position to discuss Darren's treatment in a more knowledgeable way.

You could have looked it up in a textbook – but it only merits a single line mention in the one you have in your surgery – and that book is now at least 12 years out of date.

See the Appendix on p. 247 for a list of databases with review information (you may find that they have moved from these addresses – check with the library if they are not accessible at these sites).

Fast and convenient public access to information and care through online information services and telemedicine

Many areas have points of access for anyone to access electronically provided information. Libraries have computers with Internet connections as well as experienced staff to search CD-ROMs or other portable collections of information.

North Staffordshire library service has terminals available in libraries and other publicly accessible places such as doctors' surgeries for the public to gain information about local services and welfare benefits. The North Staffordshire Health Line (01782 410011) gives health-related information between 9 am and 3 pm.

Leaflets, videos, audiotapes and interactive CD-ROMs have been used to promote health, persuade people to adopt healthy lifestyles, increase the uptake of screening and give information about specific conditions. The effort put into their production does not ensure quality or usefulness. Many are an extension of the verbal exhortations given to patients in face-to-face encounters. Giving a leaflet or video to back up information has been shown to increase people's understanding and knowledge[38] compared with just giving information verbally, but there is scant evidence of associated behaviour change.

Internet sites on health-related topics are myriad. Many of them are of doubtful value and some are positively misleading. There is a need to provide an evaluation and accreditation system to help patients make sense of the data available.[39]

Discern[40] is a project based at Oxford University to develop a system where the public can check out the quality of online health information. Another site to help people assess the quality of information is the Centre for Health Information Quality.[41]

Mrs S attends with her son, clutching a printout from the Web. It gives a short account of a new treatment entitled 'Surgical advances in the treatment of leg ulcers'. The son tells you how Mrs S has been having treatment for her leg ulcer from the district nurses for eight months; it starts to heal and then breaks down. He wants her to have this new treatment. You have never heard of it and certainly have no idea whether it is any use or whether it is available locally. You have to ask him for a copy. You can then ring your friendliest surgical consultant and ask him or her for advice.

If you want to look this up for yourself enter 'leg ulcer treatment' in any search engine; the source was: http://www.docnet.org.uk/germed/apr96/leading1.html

'Telemedicine'

Pilot studies to help overcome the distances patients might have to travel and the long waiting times for specialist opinions have used remote cameras, imaging or communication programmes. The patient is in a rural doctor's surgery and the specialist in a central hospital gives an opinion.[42] Can we foresee the future when all patients will consult their health professionals in this way?

The effective use of NHS resources by providing health planners and managers with the information they need

We need to analyse data from records to:

- look at trends and patterns of illness
- devise and use clinical guidelines and decision support systems as part of evidence-based practice
- audit what we are doing
- provide the information on which to base decisions on commissioning and management
- support epidemiology, research and teaching activities.

The collection of data must be designed in such a way that it is not only easy to enter, but is entered in a consistent way. If information is entered in different ways on separate occasions it may give unreliable results when accessed again, as in the two examples that follow.

You are looking for Rebecca Smith's records because she has apparently defaulted from her cervical smear follow-up. You find two with identical dates of birth, however, some information has been entered in one set (she lives at Willow Cottage in these and has not had a cervical smear) and some in another (she lives at 2 Water Lane in these and has had her repeat smear).

A practice decides to audit the use of aspirin as secondary prevention after a myocardial infarction. Although their patient records are computerised, information from discharge notes, hospital letters and consultations has been entered in different ways – myocardial infarction, heart attack, heart failure, cardiovascular disease, etc. It is difficult to be certain that all the codes have been entered to ensure that all the relevant records are included in the search.

Standardising entry can be achieved by:

- forms and templates to collect or analyse data
- lists and sets of terms to select, or arranging the layout of the screen to give prompts to enter data
- structured reports and referrals
- data automatically collected after entry to analyse across patient populations for audit or departmental reports
- training and feedback to standardise entry requirements.

Using drop-down lists, tick boxes and preferred terms helps to keep the data consistent – but some flexibility is needed or people avoid using the system!

Ethical and legal considerations[35]

Patient records are to:

- benefit the patient by providing a record of care that supports the clinician in the present and future
- provide a medico-legal record to support and demonstrate the competence of the clinician.

Any other use must be legitimate and implies that consent should be sought. It may include the generation of data for health service management or public health. The process of data aggregation for audit or other quality assurance programmes takes individual clinical record entries out of their original context. Misinterpretation or breaches of confidentiality may occur.

Some data collection can be misleading or faulty because the way in which the data is collected takes no account of clinical procedures. Decisions based on such data will almost always be wrong.

Korner statistics are collected about the reason for attendance at family planning clinics. The pharmacy became alarmed about the number of intrauterine contraceptive devices (IUCDs) apparently used by the clinics but not fitted in patients. Investigation revealed that the Korner statistics recorded only the first consultation, when the patient was usually given information (recorded as counselling) and a date to return for the fitting. The return visit for the IUCD fitting was not recorded in the statistics.

Sharing of information between GPs, community services and hospitals to provide seamless care

Increasingly, patients receive their care from 'teams' rather than individuals. Without the efficient sharing of information, duplication of effort or even harm may result. Ethical and legally acceptable multidisciplinary access to patient information improves care.

> Mrs S has venous insufficiency eczema on one leg and an ulcer on the other. While the district nurse is dressing the ulcer, Mrs S asks if she can have some of that Povidone dressing that her friend Mrs N has. She always has an appointment just after Mrs N and they have been comparing treatments. The district nurse is able to look up the records and is glad she did so as Mrs S has an iodine sensitivity.

The 'Child's Health Record' for shared recording of encounters with children has been a great success with parents.[43] Parents bring the book to many health professionals and the comments or queries can be seen by all involved in the care of the child, including the parents. They have a record of the child's developmental checks, the written back-up of the advice from the health visitor, and sometimes even reports from the GP. The involvement of the GP has been neglected and many do not understand the purpose or usefulness of the record.

The shared care record for the pregnant woman has an even longer history, but is often only filled in by the midwife. Again insufficient thought has gone into what use other health professionals might make of it.[44]

A pilot study of patient-held records in the care of stroke patients[45] raised some interesting difficulties. They commented that it was doubtful whether a shared record could overcome the fundamental differences in the philosophies of care which the therapists reported. The therapists also complained about the time taken to complete the record and they were concerned about the effect of openness of information on the wellbeing of the patients. The last comment suggests a lack of communication and an authoritarian attitude towards the stroke patients.

Another report[46] on shared record keeping was much more positive, showing a dramatic change in the record keeping, although some duplication still occurred. Communication between team members and discharge planning were improved.

Problems can arise if two sets of records – one the patient holds and one the professional keeps – have to be completed. One or other will be neglected unless procedures for duplication of entry are streamlined and simple.

A project using a patient-held record for home care of elderly patients found that all the health professionals and carers completed the record if requested to by the patient. If left up to them, many of them complained of time constraints and a feeling that nobody else would read it anyway. Despite this, all involved with the care found that they understood better what care the patients were receiving and that there was a reduction in duplication of clinical effort and social care. The patients were the most enthusiastic, feeling more in control of their lives. However, six months after the project finished, almost no patient-held records were being completed.

It is difficult to maintain changes especially if they involve extra effort or thought. Health professionals need to think of ways in which patient-held records could be produced more simply.

With increasing computerisation of records, it should be possible to give the patient a printout of the information he or she would like to have. This would save time, prevent duplication, and increase autonomy and self-management. A smart card with variable levels of access determined by the patient would be even better.

Further reading

- Gillies A (1999) *Information and IT for Primary Care*. Radcliffe Medical Press, Oxford.
- Kiley R (1999) *Medical Information on the Internet* (2e). Harcourt Publishers, London (includes free CD-ROM).
- Tyrrell S (1999) *Using the Internet in Healthcare*. Radcliffe Medical Press, Oxford.

Some ideas on who should do what to create reliable and accurate data in your practice

The GP

- Take ultimate responsibility for the security and standard of record keeping.
- Improve the reliability and accuracy of data recording in the practice by overseeing that there are efficient practices and procedures.

The practice manager

- Devise and organise systems to reduce duplication of data recording.
- Manage the computer system so that it is effective and offers health professionals ready access to patients' records.
- Identify staff learning needs with respect to IT and organise training as appropriate.

The practice nurse

- Be consistent in keeping accurate records for all patients in your care.
- Cooperate with the community nurses over shared care and patient-held records.

The receptionist

- Take care to maintain confidentiality when handling patients' records.
- Be meticulous about entering data in the right records at the right time.

Other attached staff: district nurse, health visitor, community psychiatric nurse, the therapist

- Access medical records in practice on a 'need-to-know' basis.
- Devise and use shared care records.

Action plan: reliable and accurate data

Today's date: ....   Action plan to be completed by: ....

Tackled by	Identify need/assess problem	Plan of action: what will you do?/by when?
Individual – you		
Practice team – you and your colleagues		
Organisation – your practice		

Evaluation: reliable and accurate data

Complete as evaluation of progress by ....

Level of evaluation: perspective or work done on this component by	The need or problem	Outcome: what have you achieved?	Who was involved in doing it?	Evaluated: • by whom? • when? • what method was used?
Individual – you				
Practice team – you and your colleagues				
Organisation – your practice				

Record of your learning about 'reliable and accurate data'

Write in topic, date, time spent, type of learning

	Activity 1	Activity 2	Activity 3	Activity 4
In-house formal learning				
External courses				
Informal and personal				
Qualifications and/or experience gained				

MODULE 5

Evidence-based practice and policy

Effectiveness is the extent to which a treatment or other healthcare intervention achieves a desired effect. 'To be reasonably certain that an intervention has produced health benefits it needs to be shown to be capable of producing worthwhile benefits (efficacy and cost-effectiveness) and that it has produced that benefit in practice.'[47]

Evidence-based care is the 'conscientious, explicit and judicious use of current best evidence in making decisions about the care of individual patients. The practice of evidence-based medicine means integrating individual clinical expertise with the best available external clinical evidence from systematic research'[48] into everyday work. Clinical effectiveness is successful when linked to local needs and priorities, so long as clinicians, managers, policy makers and patients are all involved in the process.[49]

The evidence base justifying health policy and management decisions in relation to a particular service is just as important as the evidence base for the clinical care component of the service or the education of staff providing that service.

A public opinion poll or demonstrable population need[50] could provide sufficient evidence to justify why you should provide one service rather than another. These principles are encompassed in the philosophy of clinical governance.

Incorporating research-based evidence into everyday practice should promote effective working and improve quality. The clinical governance culture is all about seeking ways to adopt proven effective practices and replace those that are less effective or more costly.

Topics included in this module

- Getting evidence into practice
- Measuring clinical effectiveness
- Evidence-based patient education
- Better information improves patient care
- National Service Frameworks are evidence-based
- Establishing and agreeing local guidelines

Getting evidence into practice

'Unless research-based evidence and guidance is incorporated into practice, efforts to improve the quality of care will be wasted. Implementing evidence may require health professionals to change long-held patterns of behaviour.'[51]

To bring about a change and get evidence into practice:[51]

- consider what individual beliefs, attitudes and knowledge influence professionals' and managers' behaviour
- be aware of important influences in the organisational, economic and community environments of practitioners
- identify factors likely to influence the proposed change
- plan appropriate interventions: 'multi-faceted interventions targeting different barriers to change are more likely to be effective in achieving change than single interventions'[51]
- interventions targeted at overcoming potential barriers are more likely to be effective
- keep people informed by describing the evidence and need for change in words and ways they can comprehend
- motivate people to tackle the change – show why the change is necessary and important, who else supports the change, how problems associated with the proposed change can be solved
- provide adequate resources to underpin strategies to change practice – such as people to promote that change who have the right level of knowledge and skills
- incorporate monitoring and evaluation of the change from the planning stage and throughout the activity
- implement the change and find ways to maintain and reinforce the new practices, e.g. reminder systems, educational outreach programmes
- disseminate information about the change in ways that are appropriate to the nature and setting of the participants.

Using the British Hypertension Society guidelines for the management of hypertension in practice[52,53]

A GP described these guidelines as being sufficiently clear and easy to use so that all the professionals in his practice were willing to adopt them. The practice team were motivated to change their management behaviour because they realised that they were not providing uniformly good care for people with hypertension. They were discriminating against some elderly patients, they were not undertaking thorough evaluation of all patients with hypertension prior to starting treatment, nor carrying out routine checks such as of the urine for protein. Implementation of the guidelines which are based on research evidence of best practice, has changed the team's clinical behaviour so that they now provide systematically good care to hypertensive patients and have a more rational approach to prescribing.

Measuring clinical effectiveness

Measuring clinical effectiveness requires you to work systematically through these stages:[23]

- Asking the right question – framing it so that it is simple, specific, realistic, important, capable of being answered, owned by those involved, implementable, focused on an area where change is possible.
- Finding the evidence: searching in the published literature, asking experts, etc.[54]
- Weighing up the evidence: as applied to your question in relation to your situation.
- Applying the evidence in practice: involving others, linking practice and policies or strategic plans, getting ownership from work colleagues and managers, overcoming barriers to application.
- Evaluating changes: making refinements to the application of evidence and continuing to monitor performance.
- Applying clinical effectiveness in the wider context of clinical governance.

Some ideas on measuring clinical effectiveness of contraceptive services in your locality

- Evidence-based practice: are you and others basing the decisions you make and types of contraceptive services you provide on best evidence?
- Consistent messages: does everyone with whom a particular client comes into contact give her or him the same information? This might include a doctor and nurse and receptionist at the clinic or GP practice, the attached health visitor, the pharmacist, the school teacher, the school nurse, parents, the local newspaper or local radio station.
- Good communication: do those from whom clients (users and potential users) seek advice, give out accurate and valid information in an easily understandable form?
- Decision making: are clients informed/involved as equals in decision making about their treatment and management?
- Appropriate methods: are the best methods of contraception being used for clients with particular needs or differing circumstances (e.g. physical or learning disabilities)?
- Good follow-up: is there good liaison between the doctors and nurses working in the local district's family planning clinics and those working in GP surgeries?
- Are you reaching those who have particular difficulties in accessing healthcare, for instance those living in rural locations or who are looked after by social services?
- Are you in contact with other people or agencies who are responsible for young people's welfare or for providing contraceptive services, such as community development workers, schools, youth workers, the local health promotion department?

Evidence-based patient education

Patients:

- want more information and seldom ask questions
- have difficulty remembering more than a few different messages at a time
- have different learning styles – some prefer written, spoken, audio, etc.
- have different language, reading and comprehension abilities
- have various life and health experiences.

So ... any patient education materials have to be sufficiently simple and flexible in the way they are presented to fulfil a wide variety of needs for information and education.

Effective patient education programmes:

- reinforce desired outcomes and behaviours
- offer patients feedback on performance
- individualise materials to patients' wants, needs and preferences
- facilitate patients taking action for themselves
- are relevant to the patient's current problem
- allow patients to express negative thoughts and reactions to what is proposed
- help patients feel in control.[55]

Patients' preferences must be considered alongside evidence-based care. Decision analysis can be used to particularise evidence to an individual patient's clinical circumstances and then individualise their management according to that patient's values and preferences.

Information about the effectiveness of a treatment for patients might include:[56]

- the likely effects of a particular intervention
- comparative risks and benefits of one intervention with others
- lay valuations of different outcomes
- clear presentation of probabilities and uncertainties
- discussion of individual applicability
- appropriate inclusions and exclusions – justify range of interventions, options included
- discussion of professional and circumstantial biases

Patients seek information on the Internet

Patients use the worldwide web to obtain information as a supplement or an alternative to consulting doctors. Reasons for searching the Web for information that were given in one study were:[57]

- information-seeking behaviour to compensate for feelings of helplessness about having an illness
- a lack of trust in own doctor, an opportunity to ask questions anonymously
- doctor had not given adequate information
- person felt ill-informed
- to find out more about others' illnesses.

▼

Better information improves patient care

Patients ought to be well enough informed to be in a position to make rational decisions about their health. The better the information patients receive, the better able they are to participate in making decisions about their own clinical management and alternatives. There is some evidence that well-informed patients who actively share in making decisions about treatment have more favourable health outcomes – for instance in the improved control of the blood sugar levels in the care of diabetics.[58] Giving patients more information has been shown to be associated with greater patient satisfaction too as the study described in the box below shows.[58]

Giving patients more information leads to increased patient satisfaction, better compliance, and better recall and understanding of medical conditions[59]

There was a correlation between patients receiving good information at a healthcare consultation and:

- greater patient satisfaction
- better compliance – in keeping future appointments or complying with their care regimen
- greater recall of information given at a previous consultation
- greater understanding of the medical condition after the consultation
- patients being female.

Patient satisfaction was increased according to the extent of communication in the consultation.

Doctors and other health professionals are more likely to favour some patients with information above others. A study undertaken in America[60] showed that well-educated, middle-aged female patients were most likely to receive good information at their health-care consultations.

Patients' characteristics can compromise the effectiveness of interpersonal care

Doctors are less likely to involve certain types of patients in making decisions about their healthcare than others.[60] Patients who seem to have the least interaction with their doctors are:

- elderly people aged 75 years and older
- young adults, aged under 30 years old
- patients who did not attend further education
- patients from minority groups
- male patients.

Men were less likely to participate in decision making if they were consulting male doctors than if they were seeing female doctors, and participated less than women patients consulting doctors of either gender, in this American study.

Tensions between the drive for clinical effectiveness and lack of financial and manpower resources[61] were demonstrated by a review of research into multiprofessional working in nine acute and three community NHS trusts.

National Service Frameworks (NSFs) are evidence-based

The purpose of the frameworks is to improve quality of care and reduce unacceptable variations in health and social services. NSFs establish models of treatment and care based on evidence for best practice which should be applied uniformly to at least a minimum standard in every part of England. The first NSF was for mental health; others will concern major diseases and illness groups.

The NSF for mental health is aimed at adults up to the age of 65 years old who have mental health problems. It:

- sets national standards for promoting mental health and treating mental illness
- defines service models
- puts in place programmes to underpin local delivery
- sets out milestones, performance indicators, timescales
- includes health promotion, assessment, diagnosis, treatment, rehabilitation, care
- covers primary care, specialist care and other responsible agencies.

Standards of the NSF for mental health[62]

Seven standards have been set for five areas:

1   Health and social services should promote mental health for all
2   Good primary care and access to services for those with a mental health problem
3   Effective services for people with severe mental illness
4   Support and care for carers of those with mental health problems
5   Action to reduce suicides

Establishing and agreeing local guidelines

Guidelines at their best, 'assist healthcare professionals ... in more effective practice of the art of medicine'.[63] They promote effective disease management by the 'development and management of treatment programmes for specific conditions in a systematic fashion to optimise the quality and cost-effectiveness of care using the best evidence available'.[63]

If you want to establish new guidelines in your PCG or PCT you should:

1   Garner local support and ownership from all agencies and practising clinicians who will be affected by the guidelines. Consult widely – does everyone consider that the topic is important? (e.g. is it a national or district priority, is there a population need, is there evidence of variable or ineffective practice or is it likely that the proposed guidelines would prove cost-effective?).

2   Establish a working group: decide who will be involved, leader(s), objectives. Membership should include: different disciplines from primary and secondary care; public health; prescribing adviser; lay member; and managers.

3   Find the research evidence and other examples of guidelines on the topic. Look at the research bases to other guidelines. See if any well-constructed and researched guidelines can be applied to your situation and if so what revisions will be necessary for your local circumstances.

4   Agree the programme of action and the timeframe.

5   Draft materials such as algorithms, clinical care pathways, information sheets.

6   Work out the resource implications and how realistic it is to expect that additional resources will be available, from whom and from where. Plan how potential cost savings will be spent.

7   Circulate draft materials to all others with interest and responsibility in the area. Ask for constructive comments and make changes to draft materials accordingly.

8   Gain consensus for final version of materials at working group.

9   Gain resources needed to implement the guidelines.

10 Disseminate guidelines – through passive (e.g. unsolicited mailing) and active (e.g. local delivery of educational programmes) means. Skilled facilitators (maybe local clinicians) should encourage take up of the guidelines.

11 Systematically evaluate uptake, adherence to guidelines, justification for deviation.

12 Identify obstacles to change and plan how to overcome the barriers.

13 Further revise guidelines in the light of new knowledge and new research evidence. Take account of comments and suggestions from practitioners who have put the guidelines into practice.

Further reading

Eccles M and Grimshaw J (eds) (2000) *Clinical Guidelines from Conception to Use.* Radcliffe Medical Press, Oxford.

Feder G, Eccles M, Grol R *et al.* (1999) Using clinical guidelines. *BMJ.* **318**: 728–30.

Humphris D and Littlejohns P (eds) (1999) *Implementing Clinical Guidelines: a practical guide.* Radcliffe Medical Press, Oxford.

Hutchinson A and Baker R (eds) (1999) *Making Use of Guidelines in Clinical Practice.* Radcliffe Medical Press, Oxford.

Shekelle PG, Woolf SH, Eccles M *et al.* (1999) Developing guidelines. *BMJ.* **318**: 593–6.

Some ideas on who should do what to establish evidence-based practice and policy in your practice

The GP

- Act as a good role model for the rest of the primary care team with regard to adopting evidence-based practice and policy whenever possible.
- Consider whether new services and procedures will be clinically effective and cost-effective.

The practice manager

- Measure clinical effectiveness and cost-effectiveness of common services.
- Monitor the application of evidence-based practice by the clinicians.
- Interpret the meaning and implications of the NSFs for the non-clinical support staff.

The practice nurse

- Apply evidence-based clinical care in your everyday work.
- Explain the evidence for nursing care to patients and involve them in decision making about the management of their ill health.

The receptionist

- Help the practice team monitor whether they are adopting evidence-based practice by gathering data under their direction.
- Keep up to date so that information you give to patients about minor health problems is based on evidence whenever possible.

Other attached staff: district nurse, health visitor, community psychiatric nurse, the therapist

- Apply evidence-based clinical care in your everyday work, fitting in with the practice guidelines.
- Be sure of the evidence base for alternative approaches to providing care.

Action plan: evidence-based practice and policy

Today's date: .... Action plan to be completed by: ....

Tackled by	Identify need/assess problem	Plan of action: what will you do?/by when?
Individual – you		
Practice team – you and your colleagues		
Organisation – your practice		

Evaluation: evidence-based practice and policy

Complete as evaluation of progress by ....

Level of evaluation: perspective or work done on this component by	The need or problem	Outcome: what have you achieved?	Who was involved in doing it?	Evaluated: • by whom? • when? • what method was used?
Individual – you				
Practice team – you and your colleagues				
Organisation – your practice				

Record of your learning about 'evidence-based practice and policy'

Write in topic, date, time spent, type of learning

	Activity 1	Activity 2	Activity 3	Activity 4
In-house formal learning				
External courses				
Informal and personal				
Qualifications and/or experience gained				

MODULE 6

Confidentiality

The principle of confidentiality is basic to the practice of healthcare. Patients attend for healthcare in the belief that the information they supply, or which is found out about them during investigation or treatment, will be kept secret.

1   Health professionals are responsible to patients with whom they are in a professional relationship for the confidentiality and security of any information obtained.
2   Health professionals must preserve secrecy on all they know. The fundamental principle is that they must not use or disclose any confidential information obtained in the course of their clinical work other than for the clinical care of the patient to whom that information relates.

Exceptions to the above are:

*   If the patient consents.
*   If it is in the patient's own interest that information should be disclosed, but it is either impossible, or
*   Medically undesirable in the patient's own interest, to seek the patient's consent.
*   If the law requires (and does not merely permit) the health professional to disclose the information.
*   If the health professional has an overriding duty to society to disclose the information.
*   If the health professional agrees that disclosure is necessary to safeguard national security.
*   If the disclosure is necessary to prevent a serious risk to public health.
*   In certain circumstances, for the purposes of medical research.

Health professionals must be able to justify their decision to disclose information without consent. If they are in any doubt, they should consult their professional bodies and colleagues.

Topics included in this module

- Consent to disclosure
- Disclosure in the patient's own interest
- Disclosure required by law
- Overriding duty to society
- National security
- Public health
- Research
- Teaching
- Management responsibility
- Secure storage of records
- Transmission of records and information
- Verbal and written reports for teamworking

Consent to disclosure

Information given to a health professional remains the property of the patient. Generally consent is assumed for the *necessary* sharing of information with other professionals involved with the care of the patient for that episode of care and, where essential, for continuing care. Beyond this informed consent must be obtained.

A social worker rings you about the mother (Mrs M) of a client. The client has told her that her mother is confused and demented. The social worker asks for information on Mrs M's health. Can you tell her without Mrs M's consent?

The consent is valid only if the patient fully understands the nature and consequences of disclosure. If consent is given, the health worker is responsible for limiting the disclosure to that information for which informed consent has been obtained. If you pass on information (with consent) to a non-professional organisation or person, ensure that the confidential nature of the information is understood (e.g. marked private and confidential).

A voluntary organisation says it is helping your patient (Mr A) with a claim against his employer. You receive a letter from the organisation with no name on the letter, just a scribbled initial. It asks for details of Mr A's medical records to be sent to them to assist in the preparation of the case. You are aware this claim is being made. What action do you take?

The development of modern IT and the increasing amount of multidisciplinary team-work in patient care make confidentiality difficult to uphold. You should be aware that patients often underestimate the amount of information sharing that occurs.

A paper reporting patients' expectations and attitudes showed considerable divergence from accepted practice.[64] The majority of those interviewed felt that administrative and secretarial staff should not have access to their medical records. Some of the patients had reservations about other doctors, not directly concerned with their healthcare, having access to their records. They were not aware of the extent to which other health staff had access to their records.

You may need to consider explicit negotiations with each patient to establish what information they are willing to have recorded in their records.

Disclosure in the patient's own interest

You may need to give information about a patient to a relative or carer. Normally the consent of the patient should be obtained.

> Mrs B is a diabetic. Her husband is very concerned about her risk of attacks of hypoglycaemia and asks you how he should manage them. What action should you take?

Sometimes, the clinical condition of the patient may prevent informed consent being obtained (e.g. unconsciousness or severe illness).

> Mr D is admitted to hospital after a car accident. He is unconscious and his brother-in-law rings to find out if he should return from holiday to be with his sister. Mrs D has gone to the canteen for a meal. What action do you take?

Exceptionally, there may be special circumstances in which a patient should not be given medical information which could be harmful to him or her and the information is given to a relative or carer in the best interests of the patient.

> Mr Y is due for another injection of his antipsychotic medication. He believes that it is a vitamin injection to help his brain cells. He is still quite paranoid but has no insight into his condition. His wife is having difficulty coping with him. She wants to know what plans are being made for his future medical care. What action do you take?

It is important to recognise that relatives or carers do *not* have any right to information about the patient. Do not breach confidentiality by giving information without consent (e.g. do not confirm a patient's attendance for treatment or give any results of investigations to someone who states that they are a relative or carer).

Mr W rings up to ask if his wife has arrived at the clinic. She is at the reception desk at the time. You cover the receiver and ask her if you can tell her husband. She goes white and exclaims that she does not know how he found out where she is. She is due to see the community psychiatric nurse because of marital problems and is living in a battered wives' refuge. What do you do next?

Reassure young people about their right to confidential medical treatment. Fears about confidentiality are the commonest reason young people give for not attending their GP for contraceptive treatment.[65]

The needs of elderly people or people with disabilities to make their own decisions can often be overlooked. Establish what information they want to be passed on to relatives, carers, social services and others.

Mrs M's son rings saying he is worried about his mother's health. He says he brought her in for some blood tests and wants to know what you think is wrong with her. How do you handle the phone call?

Including information about confidentiality in the practice leaflet, and having notices about confidentiality displayed, helps to inform people about the standards you set. Make sure all staff understand the need for confidentiality and explain to patients each time they ask for information the rules under which it is given. Many people have not thought about the implications of asking for someone else's results or if they have been seen at the surgery.

Verbal and written reports for teamworking

Increasingly, we care for patients as one of a team. Communication with other members of the team is essential.

Staff reports at the bedside have been shown[66] to maintain less confidentiality than patients believed they had experienced. Confidentiality issues in nursing practice are discussed in a review of the complex issues that should be considered.[67]

You may need to discuss explicitly with the patient what information will need to be handed on to other members of the team. Patient-held records can help to ensure that everybody knows what information is in the public domain, including the patient.

Consider patient-held records and discuss with the patient what he or she wants recorded: patients can choose who to show them to. A blood pressure chart (with readings and medication) for the patient to take to both hospital and surgery keeps everyone informed. A template of a venous ulcer size and appearance, together with treatments, helps to prevent unsuitable treatment and monitor progress.

You should also ensure that confidentiality is not misused to exclude the patient from decision making.[68]

Disclosure required by law

Confidential information may be required by law without the consent of the patient if an Act of Parliament says it must be disclosed in some given circumstance or for some given purpose.

> Information about a patient's condition may need to be given to the Drivers' Licensing Authority if he or she suffers from a condition that may affect the safety of others, such as epilepsy or diabetes.

A court order may also order disclosure in a particular case. Failure to disclose information may then be illegal, although the health professional can still decline to do so on ethical grounds and risk the legal consequences (such as a fine or imprisonment).

If the legal requirements conflict with your ethical standpoint, seek advice from professional organisations and your professional indemnity company.

Overriding duty to society

Occasionally you may feel that your moral duty as a citizen requires you to divulge confidential information. Whenever possible you should seek to persuade the patient to give consent to the disclosure. Seek advice from your professional organisations in circumstances where others are at danger (e.g. risk of harm, or rape or sexual abuse), or where a serious crime has been committed.

> Miss B tells you that her father sexually abused her. She is concerned because he has applied to foster children. What action should you take?

National security

Health professionals should satisfy themselves that sufficient authority has been obtained (e.g. a certificate from the Attorney General or Lord Advocate) and consult professional organisations before disclosing information without a patient's consent.

Public health

Legislation requires notification of certain diseases and conditions to the appropriate authorities. It may sometimes be necessary, in the public interest, to disclose information to prevent serious risks to other people's health (e.g. communicable diseases or adverse drug reactions).

> Mr K is angry that a public health doctor contacted him at home. He had recently had gastroenteritis and salmonella was found on investigation. He says he thought his medical records were confidential. What do you say to him? And what should you have said when you saw him originally?

You should satisfy yourself that information is passed to someone who has similar regard to confidentiality (not the media!).

Research

Research may benefit existing or future patients or lead to improvements in public health. Normally, confidential information about identified patients should not be used without informed consent (*see* Module 3 Establishing and disseminating a research and development culture).

The *Caldicott Committee Report*[69] describes principles of good practice to safeguard confidentiality when information is being used for non-clinical purposes:

- justify the purpose
- do not use patient identifiable information unless it is absolutely necessary
- use the minimum necessary patient-identifiable information
- access to patient-identifiable information should be on a strict need-to-know basis
- everyone with access to patient-identifiable information should be aware of his or her responsibilities.

You should tell the subjects you invite to participate in a consultation or survey about the standards of confidentiality. You should inform them about the extent to which their identity, contact details and information they give you is confidential to you, your work team or organisation.

If you are running a focus group or other small group work, you should suggest a code of practice to the group. Seek their agreement or ask the group to formulate their own modification. The rules should include agreement about confidentiality and exactly what information may, or may not, be repeated outside the group. Establish what information may be freely repeated as long as it is not attributed to named individuals.

If researchers into information about patients approach you for data from the patients' records, you should not disclose it unless informed consent is given or that consent is not required after consideration by an appropriate ethical committee. You should not disclose information if you are aware that the patient would withhold consent.

> A pharmaceutical firm that makes dressings approaches you for information about what dressings are used by patients and for what conditions. They have a scheme to reduce costs of dressings by comparing the cost-effectiveness of two dressing protocols (their product is slightly cheaper). They want a nurse researcher to look through the notes of patients who have had dressings done by the district nurse in the last 12 months. What action do you take?

Teaching

The patient's informed consent should be obtained before sharing any personal information required for the instruction. Students should be made aware of the importance of confidentiality and its preservation. Video recording is frequently used for teaching and learning. Explain clearly the purpose, use and audience to patients and give them an unpressurised opportunity to decline or request erasure of the recording.

> Is a notice on the wall by reception stating that this is a teaching clinic or practice sufficient? What other action might you consider to inform people and make sure that they can decline without feeling that their treatment may be compromised?

Management responsibility

A written confidentiality policy document should be drawn to the attention of all staff. Access to it should be encouraged and training provided.

A named person should be responsible for updating the policy document, monitoring adherence to it and dealing with any potential or actual breaches of confidentiality.

Temporary, voluntary or work experience students should all be informed of their obligations to maintain confidentiality.

Interpreters should be used wherever possible to avoid the use of friends or relatives. They should be trained in the requirements of confidentiality.

Managers must ensure that paper and computer security is maintained and put into practice systems for monitoring and upgrading security systems.

Management, clerical and administrative staff responsibilities for confidentiality include:

- a clause about confidentiality in contracts of employment
- training in confidentiality for all staff
- a named person with whom any member of staff can discuss difficulties with confidentiality, such as emotional pressure, financial inducement, or lapses by themselves or others
- reporting physical difficulties, such as lack of privacy at reception desks or being overheard answering the telephone
- having clear rules about the handling of post marked 'private', 'confidential' or 'personal'
- explaining the reasons for requests for information from patients. Only seek the minimum of information required for the task
- shred confidential paper records.

Secure storage of records

The policy document on confidentiality should contain clear procedures for recording and storing information on paper or on computer. Safeguards against unauthorised access to either must be built in and tested. Personal medical data needs to be kept separate from financial, administrative and research data.[70]

Levels of access to data should be clearly stated and passwords to computer records kept confidential (not left on a sticky label on the computer terminal). Terminal security must be arranged so that no unattended terminal can be used by an unauthorised person to access data.

Modem security must provide 'firewall' security against unauthorised access to confidential data. Technology makes sensitive data readily available – not just to those who need to access it.

Transmission of records and information

Consider the security of fax[71] or electronic data before using this method of transmission. Do you know who will see the information at the other end?

When information is requested by telephone, do you know the identity of the person to whom you are speaking? Are you absolutely sure it is not a journalist pretending to be a medical secretary?

Think about conflicts

- Medical information is confidential – yet employers and social security officers expect a signed diagnosis if someone is absent from work through illness.

- Medical information is confidential – yet relatives expect to be informed if someone is terminally ill or suffering from a serious illness.
- Medical information is confidential – yet patients expect a full and informative letter to be sent with any request for a specialist opinion, but have reservations about secretaries or receptionists seeing their medical records.
- Medical information is confidential – yet patients give signed consent for their doctors to give full details from their records to insurance companies but expect them to withhold harmful information.[72]

If health workers are confused, no wonder patients are!

Further reading

- BMA Handbook Working Party (1988) *Philosophy and Practice of Medical Ethics.* British Medical Association, London.
- Woodrow P (1996) Exploring confidentiality in nursing practice. *Nursing Standard.* **10**: 38–42.

Some ideas on who should do what to establish confidentiality in your practice

The GP

- Be clear about how to handle confidentiality and stick to recommended practice.
- Tell patients how to access results or other information.
- Discuss patient details with other staff on a need-to-know basis.
- Do not talk about patients in public areas.
- Consult your defence organisation if unsure about releasing confidential information without the patient's authority if you are asked to do so.

The practice manager

- Include a clause on confidentiality in staff contracts of employment.
- Ensure that all staff are trained in the practice procedures for preserving confidentiality.
- Advertise how confidentiality is maintained in the practice leaflet and in posters.
- Monitor who has access to confidential records.
- Keep confidential staff records in a secure place.
- Review the practice procedures and the environment to anticipate how confidentiality might be breached.

The practice nurse

- Monitor others' access to patient records kept in the treatment rooms.
- Monitor whether conversations or consultations can be overheard in treatment rooms.
- Do not talk about patients in areas where you can be overheard.

The receptionist

- Tell the practice manager if you think that patient requests can be overheard while you are on the telephone or at the desk.
- Always check identity and authorisation before releasing information.
- Report any worries or difficulties that you have with maintaining confidentiality.
- Inform the public why you cannot release information about other people.
- Take responsibility for shredding unwanted patient information.

Other attached staff: district nurse, health visitor, community psychiatric nurse, the therapist

- Be prepared to justify your need for access to patient records.
- Keep records securely if you take them out of the practice.
- Check the identity and authorisation of anyone requesting information about patients.

Action plan: confidentiality

Today's date: ....

Action plan to be completed by: ....

Tackled by	Identify need/assess problem	Plan of action: what will you do?/by when?
Individual – you		
Practice team – you and your colleagues		
Organisation – your practice		

Evaluation: confidentiality

Complete as evaluation of progress by ....

Level of evaluation: perspective or work done on this component by	The need or problem	Outcome: what have you achieved?	Who was involved in doing it?	Evaluated: • by whom? • when? • what method was used?
Individual – you				
Practice team – you and your colleagues				
Organisation – your practice				

Record of your learning about 'confidentiality'

Write in topic, date, time spent, type of learning

	Activity 1	Activity 2	Activity 3	Activity 4
In-house formal learning				
External courses				
Informal and personal				
Qualifications and/or experience gained				

MODULE 7

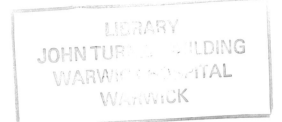

Health gain

The two general approaches to improving health are:

1   the 'population approach' focusing on measures to improve health throughout the community

and

2   the 'high-risk' approach concentrating on those at highest risk of ill health.

The two approaches are not mutually exclusive and often need to be combined with legislation and community action. Health goals include:

- a good quality of life
- avoiding premature death
- equal opportunities for health.

The Nation's Health: a strategy for the 1990s[73] sets out priority areas and detailed action plans for each. The authors list eight important general principles for public health strategies:

- partnership between public, professionals and policy makers
- coordination between different organisations
- adequate funding
- long-term planning
- recognising barriers to health promotion
- reducing inequalities in health
- education for health
- research, evaluation and monitoring.

The health gain strategy has three inter-dependent parts, all of which are covered in this module.

Topics included in this module

- Resources for health
- Lifestyles for health
- Preventive services for health

Resources for health

These are the resources needed to provide an overall effective strategy to promote public health.

Channels of communication

We need good channels of communication between local services and providers and regional or national organisations. Most of us look on committees and strategy meetings as a nuisance, taking us away from the 'real work' of patient care, but without them communication is poor.

> A local service to provide breast screening was set up in part of a now disused hospital for the mentally disabled. The uptake from social classes III, IV and V was poor.
>
> The working party met to discuss the findings and found that the feedback from non-users was that they could not get to the hospital because of poor public transport. They also felt reluctant to attend that hospital site because of its previous reputation.

Before setting up any strategy, the policy setters need to consult the service providers and the users (*see* Module 10 Meaningful patient and public involvement).

Evaluation and feedback

Policy strategy has to provide channels for evaluation and feedback. Good-quality data collection is essential for adequate evaluation (*see* Module 4 Reliable and accurate data).

Audit and research

Audit enables you to monitor whether you are doing what you set out to do. As in the example (*see* box above), you can determine which social groups are using the service. Research (asking the non-users, in this case) determines the causes of the failure to reach your audit target. An action plan (liaison with the bus company, renaming the breast screening unit) and re-audit completes the cycle of quality improvement. Research also helps you to decide what resources to utilise. In the example of breast screening, there is good evidence to support a programme of screening to reduce mortality in the age range 50–64 years.[74] Research is emerging that extension of the age range upwards is also worthwhile. Screening in women below the age of 50 is still the subject of ongoing research.

Clear governmental responsibility and liaison between departments

Accountability for public health can too easily be denied if responsibility is not clear. Communication between departments often seems cumbersome or ineffective.

> Many different government departments have a responsibility for the prevention of food poisoning, e.g. Health, Agriculture, Department of Trade and Industry, Customs and Excise, Local Government Environmental Health Officers.

Adequate funding

An adequate income for everyone is beyond the remit of health workers, but would have a major impact on public health. It is clear that inequalities of health are closely related to poverty, poor housing and poor education.[75,76] Funding for resources and services is always inadequate compared with what could be done, but good housekeeping means that new demands are subject to a value-for-money test.

Long-term commitment and programme planning

Many HImPs will not show tangible results for many years. Most avoidable diseases have many causes. Reduction in risks from one factor, e.g. high-cholesterol diets, may not affect cardiovascular disease without tackling other more significant causes, such as smoking.

Short-term interventions have been shown to lose their effectiveness rapidly. The HIV campaigns for safe sex were initially successful[77] but later evidence suggested that the effect wore off unless constantly reinforced.[78]

> Lung cancer rates follow the trends of smoking levels decades ago. Lung cancer rates in women will continue to rise for many years. Smoking cessation rates can be measured in the short term, but more realistic targets are long-term, as many people relapse. Reduction in lung cancer rates will take even longer.

Target setting

As long ago as 1985, half the regional health authorities in England and Wales had adopted numerical targets for the promotion of health. Target setting has some advantages:

- clear monitoring of progress
- a stimulus to set up accurate collection of data
- highlights key aspects of health promotion
- helping health workers to focus on activities related to health policy.

For every advantage there are always drawbacks:

- targets focus on what can be measured rather than on what is important but difficult to quantify
- targets encourage a didactic approach ('big brother knows best'), especially if imposed without sufficient public debate or education about the issues involved
- poor results from poor or inaccurate data, or unrecognised barriers to implementation, may be counterproductive
- low morale caused by penalising health workers for failing to reach targets which factors outside their control prevent them from reaching.

Examples leading to low morale

- Implementation of a meningitis vaccination programme without sufficient vaccine being available
- Giving targets for drug budgets (cost and generic prescribing) without controlling for increases in the costs of generic drugs

---

Innovations for quality improvements

The 1997 White Paper *The New NHS: modern, dependable*[4] promised to put quality at the heart of the health service. It introduced:

- the National Institute of Clinical Excellence (NICE) to promote work on clinical and cost effectiveness at national level and to draw up and disseminate guidelines
- the Commission for Health Improvement (CHI) to support and oversee the quality of services at local level
- National Service Frameworks (NSFs), evidence-based guidance to help to ensure consistent access to services and quality of care

- clinical governance in NHS trusts and throughout the rest of the NHS, backed with statutory provisions and designed to 'put quality on the agenda' of every NHS trust board
- patients' experiences of NHS care as an annual review.

The consultative document *A First Class Service: quality in the new NHS*[3] gives a fuller description of the planned changes. Health professionals and health service users have greeted the pronouncements with caution. A weakness of the NHS and changes imposed on it by the government has been the tendency to react to scandal or outrage as factors for change, rather than a systematic pursuit of excellence.

In *Improving Health Care*,[79] several difficulties with the proposed policy are outlined.

- The NICE agenda needs to include the development of evidence-based approaches to health risk reduction, early disease screening and other public health improvements. Evidence other than that generated by randomised controlled trials may need to be considered to prevent bias in the development of service provision.

- Little information exists on NHS users' qualitative care experiences. The annual survey of patients' experiences may provide new information but other specific enquiries may need to be made.
- Evaluation techniques are unreliable and new ways of assessing performance need to be developed. Effective self-help instruments for improving the performance of healthcare organisations, units and professionals should be developed.
- The expectations of better services conflict with tight financial controls.
- Over-regulation undermines the ability of health professionals to do their jobs properly.
- Quality management is not free.
- Obtaining opinions from patients' representatives is not the same as giving individuals opportunities to participate fully in improving their personal health. Better self-care is the basis for almost all good healthcare.

Lifestyles for health

The idea that prevention is better than cure is commonly held by the public and by healthcare professionals.

Changing behaviour

What about telling people to change their behaviour? Is there any evidence that it works? A study from the USA[80] indicated that drug prevention programmes targeted towards teenagers could produce meaningful and long-lasting reductions in tobacco, alcohol and marijuana use. Using data on the whole sample of 3597 students, the effects of both intervention programmes were to reduce cigarette consumption significantly – a reduction of 6% from 33% to 27% using cigarettes in any month. The proportion smoking 20 cigarettes a day was reduced by more than 20%. There was no difference in overall alcohol use, though problem drinking was reduced significantly by 6%. There were only slight differences in marijuana consumption.

Viewed by the overall results alone, the gains of prevention interventions may seem small. However, these results were obtained six years after the intervention and show powerful and long-lasting effects of an intensive and thorough prevention programme incorporating social skills training. Even modest gains spread over a large population can have immense health gains for society and individuals.

It was notable that the programmes had a much greater impact in the subgroup that attended more than 60% of the classes. Heavy smoking, heavy drinking and polydrug use were reduced by very large amounts: 25–66%. These are large health gains.

This study was randomised, intensive and had a long period of follow-up. All those involved in the design and implementation of health prevention programmes should read this study.

Do you still think people do not change their behaviour as a result of your efforts? Have a look at the Cochrane review on the effectiveness of advice for smoking cessation.[81]

Individual efforts of advice on smoking cessation targeted at health service users need to be coupled with population-directed health promotion activities. These include governmental measures such as taxation, control of sales, health warnings, control of advertising, funding for health promotion and smoking cessation programmes. Media coverage should include free comment on the dangers of smoking without undue pressure from advertisers, and fictional characters should reflect the increased majority of non-smokers in the population.

Local policies on non-smoking at work have proved to be highly successful and could be extended to more social gatherings.

The evidence for health gain for smoking cessation is clear. Other lifestyle changes are not so obviously beneficial. Diet, physical activity, alcohol intake or sexual behaviour may all require lifestyle advice. Do you have the evidence on which to base your advice?

At what level do you start to advise people to lower their intake of alcohol: 21 units per week or 30 units? Perhaps you think two units a day is optimal?

Looking for the evidence of health gain

You could attend a course to obtain a health promotion qualification, or you could read it up.

- Browsing often turns up interesting titbits of information that you can use – it's enjoyable and can be done in odd moments.
- Reading to answer a specific question is more difficult but more productive. Look at the schema below.
- Systematic research reading needs skill. Ask for help from a librarian to do a computer and hand search of the literature if you are not experienced.

A good way of looking for evidence that is important to you and your patient is to use an encounter with a patient (*see* Figure M7.1).

Good places to look for information for evidence of health gain are:

- Bandolier (www.jr2.ox.ac.uk/bandolier/subind.html)
- The York Centre for Effective Health Care (www.york.ac.uk/inst.crd)
- The Scharr site, which lists many others (www.shef.ac.uk/~scharr/ir/netting.html)

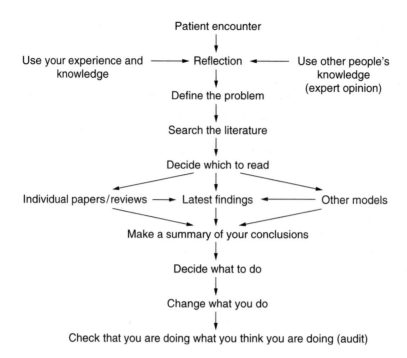

Figure M7.1   Looking for evidence of health gain.

Preventive services for health

Early detection of cancer

We use screening tests to try to detect illness before it develops. Wilson's criteria[82] helps us to decide whether screening is worthwhile (a useful mnemonic from Clarke and Croft[83] appears in the box below).

Wilson's criteria for screening: TRAP WILSON

Treatable condition
Resources for screening and treatment available
Activity must be continuous
Audit cycle continued
Protocols needed for a clear policy on when to treat

Worthwhile (cost versus benefit)
Important to individual and community
Latent phase exists for detection before disease develops
Suitable and acceptable test
Outcome improved by detection
Natural history well understood

It is useful to take an example of a screening test and find the evidence that it fulfils the criteria.

You may be prompted to do so by a challenge from a patient or colleague about the usefulness of what you are promoting (*see* Lifestyles for health section above).

You will need to do a search of the literature to establish what evidence is available. You may find a paper commenting on the anxiety caused by screening.[84] This short paper makes you think again about the way in which results are communicated to patients and you might decide to design a new leaflet to back up your advice.

Mrs Y refuses to have any more cervical smear tests. She has had three mildly abnormal results followed by a normal colposcopy result. She says the test is a waste of time and makes her too anxious. One of your colleagues agrees with her but you have recently seen someone with cervical cancer who had defaulted from follow-up cervical smears. How do you respond?

Another paper on the natural history of cervical cancer[85] might help you to explain to patients and colleagues the difficulties of using a test when the natural history is poorly understood.

Uptake of screening

While looking for specific evidence on anxiety in cervical screening and its usefulness, you notice that variations in uptake are not just due to opinionated colleagues or anxious patients.

Detection may fail because:

- people are not invited
- people are invited but do not attend (*see* box below)
- the cancer developed after the test (an interval cancer)
- the test did not pick up the cancer (false negative either because of failure to take the sample from the area of the cancer, or because the test result was read incorrectly).

Non-attendance for screening

Many women do not attend their general practice for cervical screening because they:

- want a woman to examine this private part of their body
- have had a previous poor experience with an inexperienced or unskilled health professional
- perceive the general practice to be too busy with illness
- do not understand what the test is for
- are afraid of the test
- associate cervical cancer with current sexual activity or promiscuity and not relevant to themselves
- do not want to tell their employer that they need time off or what they need it for.

Remember that any screening test is useless if you cannot get in touch with the patient to give them the result. A positive result and a patient who cannot be contacted is a worrying responsibility for the health professional who took the screening test.

Priority groups for prevention of illness

You may be prompted to examine your working practice by:

- a critical incident. For example, a patient is unexpectedly admitted to hospital, develops a complication or dies

---

Mrs S has type 2 diabetes. She is only 49 years old, but consults you about retirement on medical grounds because she can no longer see well enough to do her work. Has there been a failure of care or is she just unfortunate?

- a complaint

A man suffering from a schizophrenic illness is found dead in his lodging. His parents complain that no one took any notice of their concern that he was deteriorating.

- adverse criticism from colleagues

A league table of preventive aspirin prescribing in your PCG/PCT shows your practice is at the bottom.

- adverse criticism from authority figures

> The Prescribing Lead criticises the ratio of your prescribing between preventive and relieving therapies for asthma.

- an audit that shows poor compliance with national or local guidelines

> Only half of your asplenic patients have had a pneumoccocal immunisation.

- the introduction of new techniques, appliances or drugs.

> A new treatment for early dementia is approved by NICE. You have to instigate a screening procedure for early dementia.

Examples of priority groups for prevention of illness for health gain

1 Diabetes

Check the Cochrane Review on diabetes care.[86] Diabetes is an increasingly common, chronic condition that affects many systems and carries with it a high risk of serious morbidity and mortality. Outcomes for people with diabetes can be improved through regular surveillance and screening for the development of complications. The review reports a study in Cardiff which showed that patients who were *not* subject to prompted recall and reviews did less well after five years. Many patients in primary care default from follow-up. The review supported the view that an organised system of call and review of diabetes by family doctors can be as good or better than hospital outpatient care, and may be more cost-effective. It was also more popular with patients. Different standards of diabetic care might be a subject for a general uplifting within a PCG or PCT to those of the best results. The health gains could be considerable.

Look at the contributions from everyone in the team concerned with diabetic care:

Team member examples	Current involvement	Future involvement	How to achieve this	How will you know you have achieved it?
Patients	Passive	Active participation; greater understanding	Patient survey; focus group; feedback; patient-held records	Repeat patient survey or focus groups
Practice administrator	None	Negotiating for specialist staff or increased resources	Data collection; team meetings; feedback from staff and patients	Increased team awareness; better resources
Receptionist	Making appointments	Calling up patients for regular review	Paper or computerised diabetic register; recall standards	Audit of recall; team meetings
Practice nurse	Intermittent surveillance of patients	Regular structured care	Standardised protocol for care; education	Audit of standards; team meetings
Diabetic specialist nurses	Intermittent contact with patients	Improved liaison with practice nurse and doctors providing a specialist resource	Involvement in education; development of protocols and setting standards; input into practice diabetic clinic at intervals	Audit of standards; team meetings
GPs	Crisis intervention	Prevention of crises by structured care	Critical incident analysis; protocols for care; education	Audit of standards; team meetings
Other staff, e.g. chiropodists, optometrists, dieticians	Independent action	Coordinated care	Involvement in the structured care on or off the premises	Audit of patient care standards

2 Asthma

Effective audit showed that the number of asthma consultations with GPs fell and the number of days lost from work or school were significantly reduced after the introduction of a nurse-run asthma clinic.[87] What is done in an asthma clinic may vary widely. A similar exercise to that proposed for diabetes (above) might be useful but fewer individuals are involved in their care.

Reflection of the standards of care with a review of the literature might pinpoint some changes necessary. Keeley[88] identified some key points for failure:

Key points	Action to consider
1 Failure to identify symptoms – using structured closed questions such as 'How often do you wake up at night wheezing?' works better than 'How's your asthma?' The latter question may elicit the response 'Fine'!	A structured proforma of assessment questions. You could use a stamp on the paper record or a template on a computer
2 Bronchodilators are sufficient treatment	Compare the ratio of bronchodilator to corticosteroid inhaler prescribing
3 Failure to use corticosteroid inhalers because of steroid side effect worries	Education about the risks
4 Insufficient dosage of bronchodilators in acute attacks	Education about the correct dosages and use of spacer devices
5 Poor inhaler technique	Include a prompt to check the technique at review
6 Inconsistent advice	Consistent updating for all the team; a written management plan for each patient
7 Failure to understand the patient's point of view	Ask for feedback from the patients or carers; use a questionnaire or a focus group

Comparisons between practices in a PCG/PCT can identify specific problems and the action needed. Think about using an audit tool common to the group.

Consider ensuring that all the nurses supervising asthma care are appropriately trained. In one study, nurses without advanced asthma qualifications were significantly less confident in being responsible for patient management.[89]

3 Secondary prevention of myocardial infarction

Patients are discharged from hospital after a myocardial infarction on a variety of regimes. Take a critical look at the management and follow-up.

Management	Action
Aspirin[90]	Audit to check all patients are receiving aspirin unless contraindicated
Cholesterol[91]	Audit to check patients have had a test and what their risk factors are Check to see if their records show the risk and the advice given
Exercise testing	Is there a protocol for this? Liaise with the cardiologists for a coherent policy
Exercise programme	Is there an exercise programme? If not, how can it be instigated? Draw up a protocol for referral to an exercise programme
Betablockers[92]	Do the cardiologists vary in their practice? Can you get a consensus for the use of betablockers?
ACE inhibitors[93]	Trials have shown a benefit for selected groups of patients. Is there a consensus between practices and cardiologists?
Smoking cessation	Do you know if people need help with this? Do you know what help they can get? What do you offer them?
Angiography	Is there a protocol and consensus between the cardiologists for this?

The PCG or PCT might wish to collaborate with the hospital consultants to draw up a consistent management plan.

4 Mental health National Service Framework

Following the publication of the NSF for mental health[62] you may want to examine how you meet the criteria. The guiding principles are to give accessible, accountable, safe, high-quality, well-coordinated, non-discriminatory care involving service users and carers, which offers choices to all.

Criteria	Action
Accessible care	Survey patients and carers to discover if they know who and how to contact if their condition deteriorates. Consider a contact card listing the agencies and individuals involved
Quality	Identify the danger signals indicating deterioration. Consider giving a written guide to the patient or carer
Safety	Involves both of the above
Coordination	Patients are seen by a number of different people and agencies and are not sure who they are or what they do. A contact card could inform not just the patient
Choices	You might be able to offer a person with depression a counsellor, a community psychiatric nurse, a general practitioner, a practice nurse, a psychiatric team assessment, a place in group therapy or in a voluntary group. Practically, you may be able only to offer one of these because of the skills and facilities available in your locality

What about finding out whether what you *think* you do is actually done? Set your standards for reasonable care, e.g. how quickly someone with moderate or severe depression should be seen by yourself and after referral, and audit it. If it does not match up to what would be reasonable, what can you do? Can you lobby your PCG or PCT for more resources for your practice or improvements in secondary care? Of course, you must re-audit to see if your action has made any improvements.

Some of the standards are almost impossible to audit. For example, the first standard to 'promote mental health for all and combat discrimination against individuals and groups with mental health problems' sounds more like a 'mission' statement than a standard that can be audited.

Other NSFs will be emerging. Set up a review procedure so that you can cope with them as they emerge.

Local priorities

A local priority might be how to improve the quality of care for people with leg ulcers. Leg ulcers affect the lifestyle of the sufferers and are time-consuming for nursing staff. Dressings are a large proportion of expenditure on the drug budget.

- Find out the concerns of the patients and carers with a questionnaire or interviews.
- Establish and improve the level of knowledge of the patients and carers, the doctors and nurses with group meetings.
- Examine your working practices and compare them with others in the locality. You could compare all of them with examples of best practice[94] (or poor practice for what to avoid[95]) from elsewhere and plan improvements.
- Consider patient-held records, diagrams for the progress of healing and a form with check boxes to complete at each attendance to standardise recording and make care easier to audit.
- Discuss how you can bring the patients to you rather than the district nurse visiting at home.
- Audit and identify problems, put your action plan into place and re-audit.

A priority for your workplace may be the high number of people with back injuries. Avoidance of back injuries would result in considerable health gains. An investigation may identify particular concerns, such as poor working practices, people working alone when they should have a partner, difficult working conditions such as stores kept above head height. Preventive measures need to be brought in and monitored.

Think about others you might involve – the physiotherapist could run a back education class, the health and safety officer could make recommendations about working conditions, an occupational therapist could advise on aids for lifting, your manager could alter the working rotas to ensure that no one is lifting alone.

Identify other local priorities by patient feedback, audit and team meetings.

Further reading

Look at Module 5 Evidence-based practice and policy, Module 8 Coherent teamwork and Module 10 Meaningful patient and public involvement.
    Also:

- Mullen P and Spurgeon P (1999) *Priority Setting and the Public*. Radcliffe Medical Press, Oxford.
- Chambers R (1999) *Involving Patients and the Public*. Radcliffe Medical Press, Oxford.

Some ideas on who should do what to achieve health gain in your practice

The GP

- Incorporate national priorities like the new NSFs into practice working.
- Learn new ways of influencing behaviour.
- Focus on improving access for high-risk patients.
- Be sure that nurses to whom you delegate clinical care are adequately trained to accept the tasks and responsibilities.

The practice manager

- Identify the changes needed when new procedures are introduced.
- Identify staff training needs when change occurs.

The practice nurse

- Develop more sophisticated approaches to modifying patients' risky lifestyle behaviour.
- Keep good records so that you can remind at-risk groups about follow-up if they default.
- Develop protocols for devolved care.

The receptionist

- Help to identify at-risk groups.
- Be flexible when high-risk patients ask for an appointment or prescription.

Other attached staff: district nurse, health visitor, community psychiatric nurse, the therapist

- Know what the practice protocols cover.
- Be familiar with practice priorities and think out your role in responding.
- Refer high-risk patients back to the GP as appropriate.

Action plan: health gain

Today's date: .... Action plan to be completed by: ....

Tackled by	Identify need/assess problem	Plan of action: what will you do?/by when?
Individual – you		
Practice team – you and your colleagues		
Organisation – your practice		

Evaluation: health gain

Complete as evaluation of progress by ....

Level of evaluation: perspective or work done on this component by	The need or problem	Outcome: what have you achieved?	Who was involved in doing it?	Evaluated: • by whom? • when? • what method was used?
Individual – you				
Practice team – you and your colleagues				
Organisation – your practice				

Record of your learning about 'health gain'

Write in topic, date, time spent, type of learning

	Activity 1	Activity 2	Activity 3	Activity 4
In-house formal learning				
External courses				
Informal and personal				
Qualifications and/or experience gained				

MODULE 8

Coherent teamwork

The importance of good teamwork has been emphasised in many recent government documents.[4,17,96]

Teams do produce better patient care than single practitioners operating in a fragmented way.[97] Effective teams make the most of the different contributions of individual clinical disciplines in delivering patient care. The characteristics of effective teams are:

- shared ownership of a common purpose
- clear goals for the contributions each discipline makes
- open communication between team members
- offering opportunities for team members to enhance their skills.

A team approach helps different team members adopt an evidence-based approach to patient care – by having to justify their approach to the rest of the team.[97]

The experiences of teamwork on the Wirral[97]

The team was composed by including a family support worker employed by the voluntary sector into a community psychiatric nurses team. They found that the factors that helped the team to work well were:

- that each member of the team had a separate function
- joint training helped to cement the team; but obstacles from different employer arrangements had to be overcome
- interdisciplinary differences of opinion about patient care were welcomed as a way of increasing debate and generating a wider range of options for care.

Topics included in this module

- The place of teamwork in the vision for primary care
- Teamwork will be necessary to deliver clinical governance
- Effective teams
- Characteristics of good teamworking
- Good communication in teams
- Integrated teams
- Team building
- Skill mix
- How well is your team functioning?

The place of teamwork in the vision for primary care

The themes[98] that are emerging as a future vision of healthcare delivery are centred on teams with:

- boundaries between primary and secondary care disappearing
- more integrated care
- more user-friendly primary care (as is being developed through NHS Direct, Walk-in centres, booked admissions projects)
- easier access to primary care
- an increased range of healthcare services provided by primary care practitioners in primary care settings
- an increasingly multidisciplinary primary care workforce
- nurses with extended skills, responsibilities and training
- continuing gatekeeping responsibilities in primary care
- greater integration between health and social services planning and provision.

Effective teamwork between people working in health and social services, the voluntary sectors and non-health organisations will be needed to implement this vision. Service and education budgets of different organisations may need to be pooled to some extent to support this vision of multiprofessional teamworking.

Teamwork will be necessary to deliver clinical governance

The NHS Executive sees multidisciplinary teams working across agencies as the way that clinical governance will be practised at a service level.[8]

An integrated approach to teamwork ... to provide seamless care[98]

'Today, many patients' needs derive from chronic diseases which require care from a range of health professionals working in different organisations in a locality. Obvious examples in which there is an integrated approach between primary and secondary care are diseases like diabetes mellitus, asthma and epilepsy. High-quality care should be characterised by multisectoral, multiprofessional care delivered in a way which is seamless, as far as the patient is concerned.'

Teams are central to the Royal College of General Practitioners'[99] philosophy of how clinical governance should be applied in practice.

Protecting patients:[99]
- registration/revalidation of professional qualifications
- identifying unacceptable variations in care and areas in need of improvement
- managing and minimising poor performance in colleagues
- risk management.

Developing people:[99]
- continuing professional development or lifelong learning
- development and implementation of guidelines and protocols for 'best practice'
- personal accreditation
- recognising and celebrating success.

Developing teams and systems:[99]
- learning from what other teams do well
- clinical audit
- development and implementation of guidelines and protocols for 'best practice'
- recognising and celebrating success
- evidence-based clinical practice
- improving cost-effectiveness
- listening to the views of patients and carers
- practice accreditation
- through all these promoting accountability and transparency.

Many of these concepts and aspirations are not new. But putting them together as a whole and attributing lines of accountability so that clinicians and managers work together with specific and shared responsibilities for providing services is a new approach for the NHS.

Effective teams

Patients, staff, health authorities, the government ... will all have different perspectives on whether a team is effective. Team effectiveness relates to:

- teamworking
- organisational efficiency
- healthcare practice
- patient-centredness.

This is one way of looking at what different bodies mean by 'effectiveness'[100] in relation to teamwork:

Constituency	Examples of criteria for rating team effectiveness
Patients	Quality of service
Staff	Work satisfaction, pay, skill and career development
Hospitals	Appropriate referrals, communication
Health authorities	Target achievement, data collection, efficient use of resources
Department of Health	Target achievement, consumer satisfaction, efficient use of resources
Professional organisations	Quality of service, skill level/skill mix of staff, career development of staff

Teams that encourage participation are more likely to achieve a patient-centred service, to work together as a team and be more efficient.[100]

What predicts the effectiveness of primary healthcare teams?[101]

A study of 68 primary healthcare teams in the UK found that team size, tenure and budget holding status did not predict team effectiveness. The most effective teams had clear objectives, encouraged participation from its members, emphasised quality and supported innovation.

All the team members should determine the objectives for the team. Patients and carers might be included as appropriate. If the team is too large for it to be practically possible to meet together to do this, a board might represent everyone else. The board might consult all team members and set annual objectives taking into account other external priorities such as the HImP. Progress reports will give feedback on performance to the rest of the team.[101]

Characteristics of good teamworking

Your team is more likely to function well if it:[102]

- has clear team goals and objectives
- has clear lines of accountability and authority
- has diverse skills and personalities
- has specific individual roles for members
- shares tasks
- regularly communicates within the team – formal and informal
- has full participation by team members
- confronts conflict
- monitors team objectives
- gives feedback to individuals
- gives feedback on team performance
- has external recognition of the team
- has two-way external communication between the team and the outside world
- offers rewards for the team.

A team leader with a democratic style enables a team to function well[102] and encourages rather than imposes change.

Good communication in teams

Good communication is essential for good teamwork.[103] You need:

- regular staff meetings, which managers and staff endeavour to attend
- a failsafe system for passing important messages on
- a way to share news so that everyone is promptly notified of changes
- a culture where team members can speak openly without fear of being judged or reprimanded
- opportunities for quieter members of the team to contribute
- to give and receive feedback on how your role in the team is working out
- to praise others for their achievements
- opportunities for team members to point out problems and suggest improvements
- everyone to be part of, and own, the decision making.

Communication is usually poor if a team lacks stability or if single disciplines work in an isolated way. In one study,[61] some of the senior doctors were the worst offenders at failing to communicate with others in the team. Power and status issues within a team can interfere with good communication.

Innovations are more likely in teams that communicate well. Innovative teams:[104]

- collaborate
- have committed teamworkers

- tolerate diversity
- communicate well
- have practical support
- give positive encouragement.

Integrated teams

In an integrated nursing team, nurses form a team and appoint a nominated leader who coordinates the work, resolves any overlaps or conflicts over which particular members have various roles or responsibilities; the leader liaises with the GPs and practice manager over delivering care in line with the practice's objectives.[24] A detailed study of integrated nursing teams showed:[61]

Good points:
- The team was highly structured, problem-focused and goal-orientated.
- Multiprofessional practices such as note keeping, assessment, monitoring and evaluation were common.
- Team members were willing to be flexible about their roles.
- Being a team player was as important as being a member of a particular discipline.
- A learning culture was facilitated and supported by the heads of departments.

Not so good points:
- Not all nurses were clear and confident about their roles.
- Problem-solving skills varied in the team.
- Although teaching between professionals was common, nurses seemed to be excluded from a teaching role.
- It was difficult to integrate a newcomer into the team because she had a different philosophy about teamworking.

Integrated teams may not be exclusive to nurses. One multidisciplinary integrated team attributed their success to the professional:[61]

- being prepared to demonstrate their skills so that all team members could observe what each was doing
- being clear about what their role and contribution was
- being flexible about working across role boundaries where necessary.

And the benefits of this integrated teamworking were:

- *for patients*: continuity, consistency, appropriate referrals, less ambiguity, holistic information, better problem solving
- *for team members*: professional development through exchange of knowledge and skills.

> **The organisational factors that facilitate integrated teamwork**[61]
>
> An integrated team working in a rehabilitation unit attributed their cohesion to six organisational factors:
>
> * working close together
> * having a stable environment
> * being able to predict what happens
> * being a specialist team
> * having supportive management structures
> * having matching organisational policies.

Your practice may not have all these ingredients in your team; cohesion was the essential ingredient in these studies for successful integrated teamwork, so work on that first in your own work situation (*see* Module 1 Establishing and sustaining a learning culture).

Team building

When power is well-managed, it can encourage security, support and trust with frank and open discussion and negotiation – all part of *team building*.[103]

Team building starts from the top. Managers and senior clinicians should set good examples that encourage trust and respect from other colleagues. Without this, no organisation will be able to function at its full potential. This takes time, effort and consistency but you'll reap the rewards.

Teams may break down as a result of poor management, little guidance, poor communication and poor support. Games are often instigated by people who want to hang on to power, who may feel insecure or threatened by others. Power is a bargaining chip that people will try to grab, steal or manipulate. When power in any organisation is abused or mismanaged, the results will inevitably lead to a dysfunctional work environment. This can lead to the same troubles as beset a dysfunctional family – it falls apart.

Unless the difficulties are acknowledged, and the management is fully committed to the concept of team building, attempts to improve the situation are likely to be a waste of time and resources. If managers are equivocal about team building, and staff who attend team-building activities are the least influential ones who can most easily be spared, the long-term result will be that nothing will change. Failed attempts at improving team relationships will simply reinforce the staff's cynicism.

Skill mix

Skill mix is not an arrangement where a less-skilled colleague is substituted for another, or where one discipline is substituted for another, such as a nurse taking a doctor's place.

'Multiskilling', where several professionals develop their roles in generic ways, is not the same as multiprofessional working, where team members meet to discuss and understand each others' roles and responsibilities, learn together and plan team strategies. Recent examples of skill substitution are the telephone help service, NHS Direct, and the primary care Walk-in centres, all staffed by nurses providing the first point of contact in helping and advising patients.

Although most developments with skill mix have concerned nurses, some work has also been done with therapists.

▼

The integrated primary care team in the future[105] might have fewer health professionals with a more appropriate skill mix providing care. An appropriately skilled team will coordinate the different health, social and voluntary disciplines. It may have input from financial advisers, housing and transport officers and other relevant services. There could be several skilled subteams within the overarching primary care team:

- integrated nursing (e.g. practice nurse, health visitor, district nurse, school nurse, etc., with access to specialist nurses such as continence and community psychiatric nurses)

- integrated therapy (occupational therapy, physiotherapy, speech and language therapy, podiatry)
- integrated community mental health (community mental health nurses, psychologists, counsellors from health and social care and voluntary sectors; offering advice, listening time and reassurance to carers and patients)
- medical – GP and colleagues with whom patients are registered
- integrated prescribing – GPs, community pharmacists, designated nurses
- carers – family, friends, voluntary and professional
- support staff (including practice manager, receptionists, secretarial and clerical staff)
- integrated social workers (including respite, immediate and longer-term advisers)

and others who may move in and out of the team depending on the patient's circumstances:

- practical advisers such as financial, advocacy, housing, health promotion facilitator
- other independent contractors – dentist, optometrist, complementary practitioners, other private care provision.

The coordinator of care for each patient will be the most appropriate person for the particular situation.

How well is your team functioning?

Good teamwork does not just happen. Take time out as a team away from the workplace to review how you are working together. Everyone should have an equal chance of giving their perspective as to how the team is functioning.

Take the challenge below:[103]

There is good communication between colleagues at work	*usually*	*seldom*	*not at all*
There is good communication between managers and staff	*usually*	*seldom*	*not at all*
Team members' functions are clear	*usually*	*seldom*	*not at all*
Staff are proud to be working in your practice/unit	*usually*	*seldom*	*not at all*
Doctors/managers resolve staff problems	*usually*	*seldom*	*not at all*
Staff are treated with respect by doctors and managers	*usually*	*seldom*	*not at all*
There is a person-friendly culture at work	*usually*	*seldom*	*not at all*
There are opportunities for staff for self-improvement	*usually*	*seldom*	*not at all*
Positive feedback about performance is the norm at work	*usually*	*seldom*	*not at all*
Staff are well-trained for the tasks they are asked to do	*usually*	*seldom*	*not at all*
Team members' responsibilities are clear	*usually*	*seldom*	*not at all*
There is good leadership in your team	*usually*	*seldom*	*not at all*

Score: usually = 3, seldom = 1, not at all = 0.
Scores between 27 and 36: you have a well-functioning team.
Scores between 24 and 15: look at your weak areas and make plans for improvements.

Scores of 15 and below: as you have a long way to go, it may be best for you to consider using an external consultant to help facilitate team development.

Some ideas on who should do what to establish a coherent practice team

The GP

- Be a more democratic leader.
- Encourage multiprofessional working; value individual members' contributions to the team.
- Keep to the objectives set by the team; don't go your own way when it suits you.
- Join in multiprofessional learning and training with other team members.

The practice manager

- Not only understand the characteristics of effective teams but positively create those factors in your team.
- Involve all team members and keep in regular communication with them.
- Put teamwork at the heart of clinical governance.
- Arrange regular staff meetings and encourage everyone to participate.
- Give feedback and praise to team members when it is due.

The practice nurse

- Be flexible about fitting in with new requirements for different ways of working.
- Collaborate with other team members to find more efficient ways of working.
- Don't allow your status to get in the way of teamworking.

The receptionist

- Try to attend staff meetings.
- Contribute your views and suggestions – your ideas are just as valuable as everyone else's.
- Don't forget to pass on messages and news to other team members.

Other attached staff: district nurse, health visitor, community psychiatric nurse, the therapist

- Blend in with the primary care team and fit in with their objectives and strategy.
- Contribute to staff meetings.
- Agree your roles and responsibilities in looking after patients with chronic diseases with others in the primary care team.

Action plan: coherent teamwork

Today's date: ....   Action plan to be completed by: ....

Tackled by	Identify need/assess problem	Plan of action: what will you do?/by when?
Individual – you		
Practice team – you and your colleagues		
Organisation – your practice		

Evaluation: coherent teamwork

Complete as evaluation of progress by ....

Level of evaluation: perspective or work done on this component by	The need or problem	Outcome: what have you achieved?	Who was involved in doing it?	Evaluated: • by whom? • when? • what method was used?
Individual – you				
Practice team – you and your colleagues				
Organisation – your practice				

Record of your learning about 'coherent teamwork'

Write in topic, date, time spent, type of learning

	Activity 1	Activity 2	Activity 3	Activity 4
In-house formal learning				
External courses				
Informal and personal				
Qualifications and/or experience gained				

MODULE 9

Audit and evaluation

Audit is 'the method used by health professionals to assess, evaluate, and improve the care of patients in a systematic way, to enhance their health and quality of life'.[106] The five steps of the audit cycle are:

1 Describe the criteria and standards you are trying to achieve.
2 Measure your current performance of how well you are providing care or services in an objective way.
3 Compare your performance against the criteria and standards.
4 Identify the need for change – to performance, adjustment of criteria or standards, resources, available data.
5 Make any required changes as necessary and re-audit later.

For the purposes of audit, performance is often broken down into the three aspects of structure, process and outcome; this approach was recommended by Donabedian.[107]

Structural audits might concern resources such as equipment, premises, skills, people, etc. Process audits focus on what was done to the patient; for instance clinical protocols and guidelines. Audits of outcomes consider the impact of care or services on the patient and might include patient satisfaction, health gains, effectiveness of care or services (*see* Module 3 Establishing and disseminating a research and development culture).

The direction of clinical audit should be to promote:

- a clear patient focus
- greater multiprofessional working
- an intersectoral approach across primary, secondary and continuing care boundaries
- close links with education and professional development
- the integration of information about effectiveness – clinical effectiveness, cost-effectiveness, variations in practice, outcome measurement and critical appraisal skills.[108]

Topics included in this module

- An audit protocol
- Significant event audit
- Audit methods
- Quality and audit
- Audit of a service in a district
- Evaluation of audit
- Evaluation

An audit protocol (*see* Chapter 3)

Follow this protocol to help you carry out the audit on an important topic.

---

1   Choose a topic that is a priority for you. What is it?

2   What problem are you addressing?

3   How did you choose the topic?
     in discussion with other colleagues/decided on behalf of my work colleagues/the
     practice team requested the topic/topic is in the business or strategic plan/practice
     manager's recommendation/patient's or carer's request

4   Why did you choose this topic? Is it a priority topic: Yes/No

     If *yes*, is it a priority for (circle all that apply): the district's Health Improvement
     Programme (HImP), the government, the locality, the trust, the health authority, the
     PCG/PCT, patients, community, workplace colleagues, self, profession, National Ser-
     vice Framework (NSF), National Institute of Clinical Effectiveness (NICE), previous/
     recent significant event (organisational, clinical or performance), other (please
     write in):

5   Is the topic important (circle all that apply): Yes/No
     If *yes*, is it high cost, a common problem, life threatening, a population need, a routine check of everyday care or services? Is there evidence that current care is inadequate? Why else is it important to audit this topic?

6   What changes do you hope to make? Please write in:

7   Are these changes possible with your current resources and skills? Are you being realistic in expecting change? From where will you obtain any additional resources?

8   What will you do? Try to make sure that you include as many of the principles of good practice in clinical governance as possible, which are to:
     – have multidisciplinary input; involve colleagues as appropriate
     – consider the interfaces of how and where you work with other NHS professionals, the non-health sector and care settings
     – incorporate input from patients (e.g. users, carers, the public; at training, planning, monitoring or delivery stages)
     – be capable of achieving health gains
     – be based on evidence-based practice, policy or management
     – if you are a clinician or member of the support staff, incorporate input and commitment from managers to enable action to take place e.g. protected time for staff involved.

Audit action plan

•   Who will lead the audit initiative?

•   Who else will be involved?

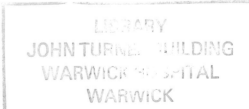

- What resources do you need to undertake the audit?

- What criteria have you selected and why?

- What standards have you selected and where did they originate from? For instance, these might be 'arbitrary' standards by agreement with other colleagues; 'gold' standards taken from published evidence of best practice; 'minimum' standards from nationally agreed levels; 'average' standards for attainment for your locality or profession; 'peer' standards being the level of performance that is acceptable to, or attained by, peers.

- What data or information will you gather as a baseline?

- When will you start? What is the timetable? Who will do what and when?

- What system do you have for reviewing the results of the audit exercise and comparing performance with pre-set standards? Who will decide and who will make any necessary changes as a result of the exercise?

- How do you compare with your peers, as individuals or other practices, as a PCG/PCT?

- What interventions or changes in services or practice will you introduce if your performance does not reach the standards that you have set? What resources will you need for these interventions or changes?

- What specific outcomes do you expect from introducing the intervention(s) or change(s)?

- How will you measure the outcomes?

- How will you demonstrate any improvements or changes from the baseline arising from the intervention(s)?

- When and how will you re-audit?

Significant event audit

See Chapter 3.

Audit methods

See Chapter 3.

Quality and audit

Quality may be subdivided into eight components: equity, access, acceptability and responsiveness, appropriateness, communication, continuity, effectiveness and efficiency.[109]

You might use the matrix below as a way of ordering your approach to auditing a particular topic.[110] There are eight aspects of quality on the vertical axis, against structure, process and outcome on the horizontal axis. In this way you can generate up to 24 aspects of a particular topic. You might then focus on several aspects to look at the quality of patient care or services from various angles.

For example, if you were carrying out an audit of your diabetic care, you might look at: (i) the process of communicating results to patients, (ii) whether patients from hard-to-reach groups such as young people have equal access to your routine diabetic clinic, (iii) whether the outcome of management is equally effective for patients attending routine GP surgeries or nurse-run chronic disease clinics.

	Structure	Process	Outcome
Equity			
Access	disease clinic		
Acceptability and responsiveness			
Appropriateness			
Communication		results	
Continuity			
Effectiveness			HbA1c
Efficiency			

Quality assurance consists of quality measurement and quality improvement. Quality assurance has been defined as 'the measurement of actual quality of care against pre-established standards, followed by the implementation of corrective actions to achieve those standards'.[111,112] Quality assurance includes medical audit and clinical audit, the quality of non-clinical components of services and the environment. Continuous quality improvement and total quality management are both umbrella terms which have become devalued over time by their multiple interpretations.

Audit of a service in a district

Just as with clinical audit, you must be sure that spending time reviewing the quality of a particular service is worthwhile. That means that your audit programme should concern an important aspect of your work that crops up sufficiently frequently to justify the effort spent on the audit.

You might audit the following.

- Range of services provided between practices – specialist services in particular settings; choice of doctor/nurse; prevention and treatment.
- Appropriateness of the services provided – extent to which services are geared to meeting local needs.
- Accessibility of services – where located, opening times.
- Information – type, options for non-English speakers.
- Publicity – extent to which the public are aware of type and availability of services.
- Skill mix – staffing levels.
- Training of staff – working within their competencies, sufficient opportunities for continuing professional development.
- Good employer practices for staff – regular appraisal, regard for health of staff at work, good communication with staff at all levels.
- Whether underlying reasons for any failure to meet standards were identified.

Examples of audit you might do on contraceptive services

Is it a priority topic? There are more than 100 000 terminations in the UK per year, and many women who are sexually active are not using contraception even though they do not wish to become pregnant.

Do we know whether and why current services are not meeting the population's needs? The published literature describes:

- Inadequate services: access and availability limited, competition between different providers (e.g. GP surgeries and local family planning clinics), inadequate training of staff, mismatch between services provided and the needs of subgroups of the population.
- Lack of knowledge of available methods of 'users' of services and non-users: emergency contraception.
- Negative attitudes: of women and men to using contraception, etc. Poor circumstances of many youngsters who have unplanned pregnancies, low self-esteem, adoption of risky lifestyle behaviour.

Setting criteria and standards: an audit project in North Staffordshire looked at the standards of contraceptive services care for young people.[113] The standard set was that all teenagers who had a live birth or termination should receive contraceptive advice.

Comparing performance with standards: 94% of teenagers who had a live birth and 47% of those who had a termination received contraceptive advice. Several teenagers reported that they had not had enough time to ask questions.

Changes were made: by hospital staff, introducing new procedures especially for teenagers being treated as day cases. Changes were also triggered in primary care and family planning clinics to provide more seamless and available contraceptive care and services.

Evaluation of audit

Evaluate your audit work to ensure that the investment of time and effort was worthwhile. You might assess whether:

- everyone participated in the actual audit measuring their performance
- everyone supported and adhered to any changes made as a result of audit
- proposed changes were implemented
- training needs that were identified were addressed
- any further audits were indicated, and if so whether they were undertaken
- the topic that was audited was important enough to have justified the effort and cost
- the method used was appropriate for the purpose of the audit
- the quality of patient care improved
- acceptable outcomes were used to measure any interventions or changes to patient care.

Evaluation

Setting up evaluation of a new service change or model of delivery is complicated by the fact that the outcome may be dependent on many factors other than your own initiative, or it may take many years to see results as the examples in the boxes below show.

Evaluating a new service that helps young people to stop smoking

You want fewer teenagers to smoke. You cannot, necessarily, attribute success to your new clinic if the rates of teenage smokers fall, as there will be other initiatives and influences affecting teenage smoking behaviour, such as peer pressure, the media and the press.

Evaluating a screening service for cervical cancer

We want to achieve fewer deaths from cervical cancer. But you cannot attribute success or blame to your particular cervical screening service if your patients are highly mobile moving around the country, the age of first intercourse decreases and if promiscuity became socially acceptable. And the effects of screening will take many years to be evident for a disease with a long lag phase in development.

A new approach to evaluation is the 'Theory of change' model.[114] It is used:

- for initiatives where there are many practitioners and organisations involved in providing services or care
- to aid partnership working
- to involve the community and take account of special problems of population groups
- to ensure that outcomes are clearly stated at an early stage.

The 'Theory of change' evaluation process raises issues that are important to all those with a stake in providing the service(s) in question. It establishes a pathway that leads practitioners and managers to agree outcomes based on a common understanding of issues, problems and community needs. The evaluation sets out measurable targets and timescales that are realistic for the particular context and problems of the population group for whom the new service(s) or project is intended. Short-, medium- and longer-term outcomes are agreed by all the 'stakeholders' at the beginning of the project.

Other ways of incorporating evaluation into your everyday work might be by:

- performance management: to check that the project or service fulfils predetermined criteria of achievement
- external review: undertaken by an independent expert
- internal review: undertaken by members of the project or service providers themselves
- peer review: undertaken by peers in your field.

Or you might evaluate your initiative or service by assessing the performance or achievement of one or more of: activity, personnel, provision of service, organisational structure, objectives.

Some ideas on who should do what to apply audit and evaluation in your practice

The GP

- Advocate audit as a useful tool for the practice team.
- Evaluate your performance and that of the team routinely.
- Make resources available for undertaking audit as necessary.
- Adhere to any changes resulting from the audit as agreed by the primary care team.

The practice manager

- Organise audit so that it is a systematic activity.
- Feed back results of audits to other staff.

- Arrange to undertake audits in parallel with other practices so that you can compare results with your peers in similar settings.
- Discuss the outcomes of the audit with others in the primary care team to gain their ownership of any changes that result.

The practice nurse

- Incorporate audit into your routine work.
- Use a variety of audit methods.
- Suggest topics for future audits when clinical problems crop up.

The receptionist

- Help by gathering data during audit activities.
- Reinforce changes by reminding others about new systems.
- Report problems for patients accessing care that may be appropriate to audit.

Other attached staff: district nurse, health visitor, community psychiatric nurse, the therapist

- Join in any audit activities in the practice at all stages.
- Feed back any relevant results of audits undertaken by your employing trust that might affect the practice team.

Action plan: audit and evaluation

Today's date: ....   Action plan to be completed by: ....

Tackled by	Identify need/assess problem	Plan of action: what will you do?/by when?
Individual – you		
Practice team –
you and your colleagues		
Organisation – your practice		

Evaluation: audit and evaluation

Complete as evaluation of progress by ....

Level of evaluation: perspective or work done on this component by	The need or problem?	Outcome: what have you achieved?	Who was involved in doing it?	Evaluated: • by whom? • when? • what method was used?
Individual – you				
Practice team – you and your colleagues				
Organisation – your practice				

Record of your learning about 'audit and evaluation'

Write in topic, date, time spent, type of learning

	Activity 1	Activity 2	Activity 3	Activity 4
In-house formal learning				
External courses				
Informal and personal				
Qualifications and/or experience gained				

MODULE 10

Meaningful patient and public involvement

You must be sincere about wanting to involve patients and the public in making decisions about their own care or about local health services for such an exercise to be successful. Real consultation involves a shift of power. Until you are ready for that, any user or public involvement in decision making will be a token event. If people feel that their opinions matter and their views are valued and incorporated in the decisions that are made they will be more likely to cooperate again in the future.

Even if those working in the NHS *want* to involve patients and the public more, the exercise may still not be meaningful if people lack the skills to do it properly.

Involvement may occur at three levels: (i) for individual patients about their own care, (ii) for patients and the public about the range and quality of health services on offer, and (iii) in planning and organising health service developments.

The phrase 'patient and public involvement' is taken to mean individual involvement as a user, patient or carer; or public involvement that includes the processes of consultation and participation.[25]

Topics included in this module

- Advantages of patient and public involvement
- Why public consultation may be ineffective
- Meaningful patient and public involvement
- Doing it right
- Planning your method
- A range of alternative methods
- Choosing the right method
- Was the consultation worthwhile?
- Feedback and views from patients

Advantages of patient and public involvement

Partnership working between the NHS and users of local health services has resulted in more efficient use of local community resources, more effective health services and more accountability for public funds.[115] Community development work in Tyne and Wear[116] has shown how the NHS may come to regard the community as a 'key asset in creating solutions' and become responsive to the community's views.

Community participation in Tyne and Wear[116]

The Newcastle Health Partnership has a strategy for city-wide community participation that aims to help local communities act on their own health agendas. Special efforts have been made to include black and ethnic minorities, gay and lesbian groups, older people, adolescents and people with a physical or sensory disability. Health priorities emerged from the 90 local groups involved in the initiative and were taken up by health services management. An annual local health conference is attended by more than 200 local people, and develops priorities for the year's proposed health commissioning.

Involving people in planning services and making decisions about local healthcare does increase their ownership of the NHS and gives them more understanding of how the NHS operates and the problems it faces. The NHS Executive regards user and public participation as an important priority for all PCGs and PCTs.

The NHS Executive[117] **believes that:**

- services are more likely to be appropriate and effective if based on needs identified together with users (and the public)
- users are seeking more openness and accountability
- patients want more information about their health condition, treatment and care
- involving patients in their own care may improve healthcare outcomes and increase patient satisfaction
- patients need access to reliable and relevant information to be able to assess clinical effectiveness themselves

---

Patient and public involvement depends on people listening and being willing to respond to the views obtained if action is to result. People need to be well-informed about the issues if they are going to be effectively involved.

Why public consultation may be ineffective

Many public consultations about health issues have been of dubious quality and not been sustained. Some of the reasons for this are thought to be that:

- public engagement initiatives may really be disguised public relations exercises
- methods of consultation may depend on practitioners' and commissioners' preferences and limited experience rather than being the best method(s) for the purpose
- there may be a lack of commitment from the healthcare unit to act on the views obtained
- unwanted results may be disbelieved as being unrepresentative of the subject population and then ignored
- decision making may be based on the historical background rather than a needs assessment or true consultation
- public consultation exercises are usually time-consuming
- the enthusiasm of the response from the public and breadth and detail of information they volunteer may overwhelm the organiser.

Other barriers to consultation include a lack of funds and a lack of clarity about how to get good public representation. Ordinary citizens may be deterred from joining in discussions about the health service on equal terms by a lack of information, lack of confidence, time, training and skills.

Little evidence of direct patient/public involvement in GP commissioning pilots[118]

Patient and public decision making within the 40 GP commissioning pilots was limited.

Using a scale measuring the extent of influence of different stakeholders, where 0 = 'no influence' and 5 = 'great influence', the 'public' had an overall average score of 0.7, 'patients' scored 0.8, 'non-lead GPs' scored 3.1, and 'health authorities' scored 3.6. The research concluded that those in GP commissioning pilots lacked the skills, rather than the will, to involve patients and the public in decision making.

Real consultation means being committed to act on the results. Many public consultations have only involved the most accessible people or groups.

Meaningful patient and public involvement

Moving to meaningful user or public involvement will not happen until there is a change in culture where those in the NHS want to engage with people and respond to their views. Many consultations at present involve the most accessible people and simply mirror the power balance that already exists in society. If a patient involvement or public consultation exercise is to be meaningful it has to involve people who represent the section of the population that the exercise is about. You must find ways to seek out the opinions of ordinary people who haven't got time to go to meetings or the inclination to fill in survey forms. People in hard-to-reach groups such as the homeless or those who speak little or no English will be most unlikely to come forward and give their views unless you use an intermediary. You will have to set up systems to actively seek out and involve people from minority groups or those with sensory impairments such as blind and deaf people.

▼

Using patients' views about the management of breast cancer in Sandwell

Twenty women who had been treated for breast cancer were randomly selected and invited to two parallel focus groups. A clinical psychologist facilitated the groups. Eight aspects of treatment for breast cancer were discussed. A main theme emerging from both groups was about the importance of good information being given to patients throughout the care process. The draft copy of the report was approved by the participating patients before the final report was distributed to staff. Findings were fed back to the clinicians to make changes to the service.

Doing it right: boring but necessary

You need to consider:

- your sampling method to ensure that you are involving a representative sample of the population who are the target of your initiative (*see* Module 3 Establishing and disseminating a research and development culture)
- validity and reliability of the method, for instance the design or content of a questionnaire, the rigour with which interviews are undertaken (*see* Module 3 Establishing and disseminating a research and development culture)
- the requirements of the Data Protection Act: that all personal data held on computer should be 'secure from loss or unauthorised disclosure'. Personal data is any information about someone else and includes information collected about named subjects
- ethical approval if your project involves patients receiving other than routine, everyday care
- statistical software: find out more about what particular statistical programme might be available and appropriate from your local university department, or the information department at your trust or health authority
- entering data is best carried out twice over; compare the tallies of both sets of results to see if there are any discrepancies between them and correct the reason for that
- informed consent: people should feel free to decline to consent to participate in the consultation without feeling that this will prejudice the quality of the care or attention they receive from you in future
- access to medical records and confidentiality: the *Caldicott Committee* report[119] found that there was a general lack of awareness throughout the NHS of good practice in confidentiality and security about patients' medical details (*see* Module 6 Confidentiality).

Patients' ability to understand and consent to randomised controlled trials depends on their education[120]

Forty middle-aged and elderly carers of patients with Alzheimer's disease were given information about research trial design in semi-structured interviews, backed by written information sheets. Three fifths of them could not explain why placebo, randomisation and double-blind procedures were used. Subjects were more likely to understand information about participating in a randomised controlled trial if they had stayed on at school or college.

The patient must be provided with sufficient information for informed consent to be truly given. The rigour of scientific method or objective evaluation applies just as much to patient involvement and public consultation exercises as any other research and development project, if the results are to be valid and reliable.

Planning your method of patient involvement or public consultation

Don't just do a survey or run a focus group because it seems a good idea or there is a requirement to do it, or it will end up as a meaningless exercise. Before you start: define the purpose, be realistic about the magnitude of the planned exercise, select an appropriate method or several methods depending on the target population and your resources, get the commitment of everyone who will be affected by the exercise, frame the method in accordance with your perspective, write the protocol. Think about the following.

- Why you are considering organising a user involvement or public engagement exercise – what is the purpose of the exercise?
- Whether the exercise really needs doing.
- What structures do you already have in place for undertaking user involvement or public engagement exercises that you might use?
- Agreeing the purpose of the exercise with all your colleagues at work who will be affected by the undertaking and the outcome of the exercise.
- Being realistic in your choice of method depending on whether you have identified resources, your practice or organisation and colleagues are behind you, you are capitalising on momentum created by it being a priority or part of a strategic plan at work or you are building on successful previous initiatives.
- Select an appropriate method for the population concerned: (i) the whole practice population or local community (users and non-users of your healthcare services), (ii) identifiable patient groups, (iii) individual patients, carers or families.

Your own circumstances will limit your choice of methods for all the reasons previously described.

City-wide consultation in Sheffield[121]

Around 5000 people responded to this consultation exercise: 1421 were individuals, 90 inter-agency groups or organisations, 11 professional groups and 92 were community groups. The aim of the consultation was to find out what people thought were the main health issues and problems affecting their health and to look for ideas about what could be done to improve health in Sheffield. The consultation methods included talking to ordinary people, groups and agencies, holding discussion groups, producing audio and written materials to inform the debate, appending a questionnaire to discussion documents. The responses were mainly written, but included phone calls, memos, audio and video taped comments and suggestions.

Inappropriate method(s) will mean patient/public involvement activities waste time and effort as well as needlessly raising other peoples' expectations about change.

> Is someone else already doing something similar? Does the information already exist elsewhere? Can you adopt their results instead?

A range of alternative methods

Different techniques may give dissimilar results if the methods used are biased or inappropriate for the purpose. If the consultation is about complex issues such as rationing or prioritising healthcare, the method should include a stage whereby the participants are informed about the topic first and have opportunities to discuss and reflect on the issues.

Some methods are more time-consuming and costly than others. A method of convenience may be cheaper in terms of resources but be more likely to produce biased views; whereas more complex and time-consuming methods may be designed to elicit representative opinions from a cross-section of the relevant population.

Questionnaires are often used – for instance, as postal or administered surveys, or as self-completion enquiry slips attached to other documents. But it is not easy to design a valid questionnaire with unambiguous questions.

The variety of qualitative methods that can be employed to gather information and views from patients, carers, and the general public include:

- focus groups – discussion groups
- interviews
- special interest patient groups: user groups, carer groups, patient participation groups, disease support groups
- general public opinion: opinion polls, citizens' juries, standing panels, public meetings, neighbourhood forums
- community development: local community development projects, healthy living centre activities, rapid appraisal
- consensus events or activities: Delphi surveys, nominal groups, consensus development conferences
- informal feedback from patients: in-house systems such as suggestion boxes, complaints.

Adapting rapid appraisal to assess health and social needs in general practice[122]

Rapid appraisal was used to build a profile of a community living on a council estate of 670 homes. The three sources of information used were: existing documents about the neighbourhood, interviews with a range of informants and direct observations. Interviews and focus groups identified six priorities for change, many of which were not directly health-related. The rapid appraisal initiative took 12 meetings of the development team and 45 interviews; in retrospect, the team thought that the first 25 interviews with 10 residents and 15 local workers would have been sufficient.

Selection of method is likely to be limited by few having the skills to undertake all the alternative methods listed above. Save time, effort and error by using a method that someone else has already tried and tested for the same purpose in similar circumstances – a validated questionnaire, a published interview schedule, a standing panel already set up by another agency.

Choosing the right method

The next stage is to decide which methods are the most appropriate for any particular situation or purpose.

The overall theme of the following illustrations is to include patient/public involvement in making difficult decisions about treatment, funding or resources.

If your purpose was: to make difficult decisions about treatment, funding or resources

Specific objectives might be to gain peoples' views in order to:

- make decisions about rationing or prioritising services or treatments – who should be involved and when
- centralise services and reduce peripheral facilities
- look at reducing costs by using less-skilled staff for the aspect of care under consideration
- find out what services patients or the general public think the NHS should provide for particular groups of people
- determine peoples' views before a new procedure is brought in, to understand their information needs and afterwards to learn from their experiences.

Examples of topics you might consider

- local criteria for funding non-life threatening medical treatments such as fertility treatments
- substitute nurses for doctors, assistants for qualified therapists, counsellors for psychologists to provide healthcare services
- whether people on waiting lists should be prioritised according to functional need or length of time waiting, for example topics such as cataract surgery

---

You might choose one or more methods of involvement from the alternative methods set out as a flowchart (*see* Figure M10.1). Start at the top, identify the specific objective of the exercise, the topic of interest and make a plan. Your choice of methods will depend on whether the group who are the target of the consultation exercise are the local community, a subgroup of the population who are difficult to locate, a specific group of patients sharing the same characteristics or needs whose contact details are readily accessible or individual people. Then you will need to think whether the type of involvement you are seeking is mainly to inform the target group or to receive information from them, or whether you are looking for an interactive exercise with a two-way exchange of information.

There may be other methods that suit your purpose not mentioned here. The information from two or three methods may be combined to give you a better picture of patients' and the public's views.

Was the consultation worthwhile?

The most important stage of a patient/public involvement or consultation exercise is listening to the views obtained and responding appropriately. The findings are more likely to be implemented if the whole exercise is part of a wider strategic plan, whether at practice, unit or organisational levels, and/or the exercise is 'owned' by the group of individuals who the results will affect, rather than being the hobbyhorse of one or two people. So a consultation might be a one-off event or part of a systematic or dynamic process.

When thinking whether the effort and expense was worth it, consider:

- whether the information was already available from other sources
- the appropriateness of the costs of the consultation process – were they in proportion to the purpose and the outcomes?
- whether the source of the resources used was appropriate for the purpose and outcome of the consultation/survey
- the extent to which the results of the consultation/survey were generalisable to other groups of people, populations, settings or circumstances, so that you get extra value for the work you've done.

Establish specific objectives
|
Agree priority topics to consider
|
Plan your involvement or consultation exercise
|
Consider selection of the following activities:

If your target population is

Practice population or local community

INTERACTIVE PROCESS

Options:
- consensus development conference
- Delphi study
- public meeting
- citizens' jury
- lay representative on board as conduit
- presentations to groups, discussions
- talk with Community Health Council
- public notices
- prize-winning competition
- advertise board meetings well to public

Patient group, patients, carers

INTERACTIVE PROCESS

Options:
- lend videos
- sit in on users' group as observer
- run nominal groups
- give presentations to users' groups
- invite comments on draft plan
- involve users in evaluating service
- patient record diaries
- hand-held patients' records

PATIENTS/PUBLIC RECEIVE INFORMATION

Options:
- hold discussion on local radio
- hold roadshow
- health information booklet to households
- work through voluntary organisations to hard to reach groups

PATIENTS RECEIVE INFORMATION

Options:
- particular patient/group give lay perspective
- create library of resources for patients
- lay people act as advocates
- organise co-ordinated cascade
- advisory notices about changes
- use other's communication system
- start correspondence in local newspaper

PATIENTS/PUBLIC GIVE INFORMATION

Options:
- set up and use standing panel
- one-off opinion poll
- focus groups
- semi-structured interviews
- neighbourhood forums
- rapid appraisal initiative

PATIENTS GIVE YOU INFORMATION

Options:
- community development project
- focus groups
- nominal groups
- face-to-face interviews
- feedback or evaluation slips

Figure M10.1   Making difficult decisions about treatment, funding or resources.

Examples of costs of various types of involvement/consultation exercises

- Citizens' jury: typical costs are quoted as being around £16 000 plus considerable staff time,[123] up to £30 000.[124]
- Neighbourhood forum, patient participation group, user group: members are volunteers. Thus the expenses will be those of organising the event, possibly reimbursing travel expenses, providing light refreshments, administration, reports or a newsletter. Such a forum or group probably costs the NHS less than £100 a meeting, the comparatively low cost being because of participants giving their time without charge.

The costs and effort of involvement and consultation exercises are wasted if maximum use is not made of the findings. Barriers to change are well known; those undertaking patient and public involvement should anticipate problems in applying the results.[97]

Some feedback and views from patients

If you just ask patients for their views about the services you offer, the information they give you will give you pointers about changes you might consider. Such an exercise in a community trust drew the following comments from a variety of patients and relatives quizzed at random.

What are the good points about the services and care provided by this trust?
- 'Easy to talk to' (about the health visitor).
- 'Good access, convenient times' (about the chiropodist).
- 'The midwives are excellent – they make you feel special.'
- 'I didn't feel as if I was just another patient' (about the midwife).
- 'Everything was brilliant – told me everything in layman's terms so I could understand what it was all about' (about the midwife).
- 'The staff are excellent – they do what they're supposed to do.'

Are there any improvements in the quality of care the trust provides that you would like to see?
- 'Health visitors are sometimes difficult to contact by phone.'
- 'Sometimes what people tell me confuses me.'
- 'The wait to be seen is too long. I have had to wait seven weeks for my appointment. I have had to buy bigger shoes because my toe is so painful' (chiropody).
- 'You get the right treatment but you don't get enough of it' (occupational therapy).
- 'Staff do their best but I have my doubts. I sit in this chair an awful long time and could be doing more' (respite inpatient care).

What do you consider is the most important issue in terms of the quality of care or services that the trust provides?
• 'Getting an appointment quickly is most important.'

What do you consider is the most important issue in terms of the quality of care or services individual members of staff provide?
• 'Responding to calls for the toilet.'
• 'Being efficient – good at their job.'
• 'Taking my worries seriously.'

Would patient like to be involved in monitoring or assessing the quality of care or services?
• 'Would like to be involved more.'
• 'Quite happy for professionals to monitor care themselves – it's going okay why change it?'
• 'Want to be able to know what care I should expect. I've not had occupational therapy for three weeks and I'm not clear whether I should be having it or if I'm not due for it.'
• 'Patients and the relatives should get involved. Relatives could give an opinion but not a judgement as they're not here all the time, so they wouldn't know how they (the nurses) work when they're not here nor what they're supposed to be doing.'

Some ideas on who should do what to establish meaningful involvement of patients and the public in your practice

The GP

• Welcome unsolicited patient views and act on suggestions.
• Set up meaningful patient and public involvement systems; incorporate patient input into decision making such as into the practice's business plan.
• Learn more about various methods of public consultation to understand which may be appropriate in given situations.

The practice manager

• Organise various methods of patient involvement and public consultation.
• Set up a health panel in the practice – for patients to respond with their views.
• Provide good information to patients about the practice systems.

- Find out if you can link the practice into others' public consultation mechanisms, e.g. the health authority, the city council.

The practice nurse

- Suggest important topics on which the practice might consult.
- Participate in consultation exercises by administering a short questionnaire to a sample of patients.
- Prepare patient literature giving information about various clinical conditions; encourage questions.

The receptionist

- Administer the suggestion box; empty it out regularly and pass suggestions to practice manager.
- Record every comment and suggestion from patients so that the practice can look for trends.
- Help with any data collection, such as administering surveys.

Other attached staff: district nurse, health visitor, community psychiatric nurse, the therapist

- Share good practice learnt from your employing trust.
- Help to identify patients with specific conditions to which a consultation exercise relates.

Action plan: meaningful patient and public involvement

Today's date: ....   Action plan to be completed by: ....

Tackled by	Identify need/assess problem	Plan of action: what will you do?/by when?
Individual – you		
Practice team – you and your colleagues		
Organisation – your practice		

Evaluation: meaningful patient and public involvement

Complete as evaluation of progress by ....

Level of evaluation: perspective or work done on this component by	The need or problem	Outcome: what have you achieved?	Who was involved in doing it?	Evaluated: • by whom? • when? • what method was used?
Individual – you				
Practice team – you and your colleagues				
Organisation – your practice				

Record of your learning about 'meaningful patient and public involvement'

Write in topic, date, time spent, type of learning

	Activity 1	Activity 2	Activity 3	Activity 4
In-house formal learning				
External courses				
Informal and personal				
Qualifications and/or experience gained				

MODULE 11

Health promotion

Different approaches to health promotion[125] include:

- medical and preventative behaviour change
- educational
- empowerment of the individual
- social change.

The Health Service is mainly concerned with the medical model that aims to reduce morbidity and premature mortality. You need to consider how you can inform patients about health risks and how you can help patients change their behaviour.

Table M11.1 summarises one model for health education.[126]

Table M11.1 Model for health education

1 Health persuasion	Interventions by professionals, aimed at individuals, e.g. advice to stop smoking or to take exercise
2 Legislative action	Intervention by professionals, aimed at communities, e.g. lobbying for legal changes in school sex education programmes
3 Personal counselling	Led by individual need, performed by professionals, e.g. professionals helping an individual choose treatments when options are available
4 Community action	Led by community needs, performed by professionals, e.g. professionals helping a group to lobby for a local resource

Topics included in this module

- Targeting
- Ethical problems
- People with disabilities
- People with learning disabilities
- Confidentiality of health promotion information
- Evaluation of health promotion
- Pitfalls of enumeration
- Pros and cons of health promotion
- Checklist

Targeting

You can target whole populations, e.g. giving advice on the prevention of depression to everyone you see *or* you can target high-risk groups, e.g. giving advice on the prevention of depression to elderly people with precipitating causes such as bereavement.

The medical approach can be criticised for ignoring the social and environmental aspects of disease. It tends to encourage dependency on medical knowledge and can remove health decisions from individuals. Health professionals need to develop strategies to encourage individual action (empowerment) and reduce attitudes of coercion or blame.

Health promotion can only be effective if patients can access the services available. Workers in the health service will be mainly concerned with activities 1 and 3 in Table M11.1. They may become involved individually in more community-orientated activities (2 and 4) on occasions by joining pressure groups, charities, or lay organisations as professional advisers, etc.

Ethical problems

The essential nature of health education is that it is voluntary. If patients attend for advice or treatment for a particular problem, is it right to include opportunistic information gathering in the consultation? Patients may not have given their *full informed consent* to these activities.

> Information may be sought as to whether patients smoke or their blood pressure may be checked. Patients are often not aware of the consequences of a raised blood pressure reading or that information on smoking habits may be given at a later stage to an insurance company.

Patients may fear that a refusal to consent to health promotion activities will affect how you manage the problems with which they have attended. You have an extra responsibility if you involve patients in these activities. See the checklist at the end of this section.

People with disabilities

Access to health promotion activities is often difficult for those with physical handicaps, visual or hearing impairment, etc. Think about how to provide informational materials other than in traditional leaflet format.

Videotapes, picture-based formats and role-play are all useful tools.

Consider how you can take health promotion to selected groups, rather than expecting them to come to you.

A health visitor, doctor, practice nurse or district nurse could attend meetings of self-help groups or run a group at a sheltered housing complex.

People with learning disabilities

People with learning disabilities have the same right as anyone else to make their own decisions. Just because it takes more time, or the information has to be explained in a different way, the competency of the patients to understand and to make their own decisions must not be underestimated.

> Break information into smaller-sized bits. Use pictures, drawings and models even more than you would usually. Give simple information sheets to take away.

Always try to seek the patient's consent to telling a carer or relative. A decision to disclose information to a parent or carer should only be taken where the lack of understanding is too great to be overcome, and should be carefully documented.

Confidentiality of health promotion information obtained during health promotion activities (*see* Module 6 Confidentiality)

Have you decided:

- who can share your clinical information?
- what information is essential for other professionals to know and what does not need to be shared?
- what information should not be given to other people such as employers or insurance companies?
- under what circumstances you can breach confidentiality, e.g. when a child is at risk or the general public good outweighs the personal protection?

> An angry patient rang. His insurance company had contacted him asking for details of his heart disease. What had the doctor told his insurers? An investigation discovered that his daughter had applied for a mortgage with the same company with whom he had a mortgage. The doctor had completed an insurance form for *her*. The nurse had recorded on *her* notes during her health screening when she had joined the practice 'FH: CVS disease (father)', and this information had been transcribed on to the insurance form. The father thought that passing on information about him on a form about his daughter was a breach of confidentiality. What do you think?

Evaluation of health promotion

Preventive measures are ultimately evaluated by a reduction in disease morbidity and mortality. Shorter-term evaluation such as an increase in the number of people being offered health promotion activities has often been used instead. Such enumeration is unable to measure any change in behaviour.

You need to consider what outcomes[127] you might be able to measure and how reliable they might be. Timing of evaluations can be difficult. An immediate post-programme evaluation may not be sustained after six months, or changes can take time to show (*see* Module 9 Audit and evaluation).

> You might record that 70% of people had given up smoking after a stop smoking course. Others might rightly criticise if you only measured this at six weeks after the course. Your desired outcome is for people to stop permanently. A better measure might be to compare the rates of cessation at six weeks, six months, 12 months and six years later.

Pitfalls of enumeration

An emphasis on evaluation has led to health promotion activities being based more on what can be measured than on effective measures that are less easily quantified. Results are interpreted differently according to the viewpoint of the receiver of the report.

- A funder of a project may insist on cost-effectiveness.
- A nurse may be looking for acceptability to the patient.
- Managers may measure success by indicators of increased productivity.
- Patients may want to increase their control over some aspect of their health.

The ideal is to be able to present all these facets in a report about a health promotion activity. A further difficulty is being sure that the changes measured are due to the health promotion activities rather than any other external change. Confounding external factors may influence your results.

> You have instigated a programme of health promotion on accident prevention among the elderly living in accommodation with a warden. You record the number of accidents involving attendance at Accident and Emergency units before and after the intervention. During this time, the local shopping centre becomes traffic-free, with ramped pavements for easy access and volunteers use a specially adapted bus to transport elderly residents to the shopping centre. The number of elderly residents attending the A&E unit falls dramatically. Which intervention has had an effect?

Evaluation is only worth doing if it will make a difference to what you do next. Interpretation and feedback to those involved must be incorporated into the design. Evaluation is not a simple activity and may consume resources that would be employed more constructively. Monitoring of activity may be all that can be achieved, but you should be clear about the differences between monitoring and evaluation.

Pros and cons of health promotion

Advantages to carrying out health promotion activities with general medical care

- Doctors and nurses have credibility. The survey by Health Education and the Consumers Association found that 95% respondents trusted their family doctor and 87% trusted the nurse.
- Other sources of information were much less trusted: radio and television 63%, newspapers and magazines only 25%.
- Local services are more accessible.
- Repeated contact builds up trust and increases opportunities for reinforcing health education messages.
- Patients often attend primary care before diseases become established. The possibilities for prevention are enhanced.
- Adding on to established provision is cheaper than providing new facilities.

> Do you think that the health professional should spend time trying to persuade a man with chronic bronchitis to give up smoking or spend the time monitoring his condition and teaching him how to use his inhalers properly?

Drawbacks to carrying out health promotion activities with general medical care

- Doctors and nurses are often not adequately trained or competent at health promotion activities.
- They should not be involved in activities designed solely to meet the demands of income generation at the expense of meeting demonstrable health needs.
- The value of health checks, regardless of health status, is not clear. There are few screening activities that have benefits clearly based on evidence rather than hope.
- Those who would benefit most from lifestyle advice are least likely to take up services on offer.
- Those who need to make the greatest lifestyle changes often have environmental constraints, such as poverty or poor housing, which are mainly susceptible to political or community changes.
- The demands of an illness service are more immediate and leave little time or opportunity for health promotion activities.

Checklist to help you think about health promotion[125]

Central considerations in working for health

- Are you enabling people to direct their own lives?
- Do you respect peoples' decisions even if they conflict with your own?
- Do you treat people equally?
- Do you work with people on the basis that those who need your help most come first?

Key ethical principles[128]

- Are you doing more good than harm?
- Are you telling the truth and keeping promises?

Consequences of ways of working for health

- Will your actions increase the health of the individual?
- Will your actions increase the health of a particular group?
- Will your actions increase the health of society?
- Will your actions have any effect on your own health?

External consequences in working for health

- Are there any legal considerations?
- Is there a risk attached to the intervention?
- Is this intervention the most effective and efficient action to take?
- How certain is the evidence on which this intervention is based?
- What are the views and wishes of those involved?
- Can I justify my actions in terms of all this evidence?

'Prevention is better than cure' is only true if it is effective and acceptable to both provider and recipient.

Websites

http://www.wolfson.tvu.ac.uk/learn/links/promo.stm is a useful website with many other links to health promotion information.

Further reading

Pike S and Forster D (1995) *Health Promotion for All*. Churchill Livingstone, Edinburgh. This book contains a framework for developing a personal health promotion portfolio.

Some ideas on who should do what to increase health promotion activities

The GP

- Incorporate reminders on patient records.
- Identify target groups for health promotion activities.
- Take opportunities to promote health proactively and record what advice has been given.

The practice manager

- Set up who does what health promotion activities in the practice.
- Support staff in learning best practice.
- Provide time for health promotion activities.

The practice nurse

- Innovate new ways of informing people about health.
- Run patient groups.
- Use templates or structured records for recording health promotion activities.

The receptionist

- Invite patients for health promotion activities.
- Publicise practice activities.

Other attached staff: district nurse, health visitor, community psychiatric nurse, the therapist

- Provide relevant educational material.
- Be aware of health promotional activities in the practice.
- Encourage patient participation.

Action plan: health promotion

Today's date: ....   Action plan to be completed by: ....

Tackled by	Identify need/assess problem	Plan of action: what will you do?/by when?
Individual – you		
Practice team – you and your colleagues		
Organisation – your practice		

Evaluation: health promotion

Complete as evaluation of progress by ....

Level of evaluation: perspective or work done on this component by	The need or problem	Outcome: what have you achieved?	Who was involved in doing it?	Evaluated: • by whom? • when? • what method was used?
Individual – you				
Practice team – you and your colleagues				
Organisation – your practice				

Record of your learning about 'health promotion'

Write in topic, date, time spent, type of learning

	Activity 1	Activity 2	Activity 3	Activity 4
In-house formal learning				
External courses				
Informal and personal				
Qualifications and/or experience gained				

MODULE 12

Risk management

PCGs and PCTs are accountable for delivering minimum standards of care through clinical governance. They will manage risk by detecting deficiencies then applying strategies that establish standards and minimise shortfalls in the provision of care and services. Good organisation and efficient practice systems should reduce the chances of mistakes happening or patients not being followed up.

Risks may be prevented, avoided, minimised or managed where they cannot be reduced.

Practice team makes clinical governance plan to improve the safety of patients who are on warfarin

Two members of a practice team attended a workshop to learn more about clinical governance. They decided to focus on risk management in the practice as an important component of clinical governance. There had been a recent critical event where a patient who had been put on warfarin for three months was still taking it two years later.

The practice team plan a range of action. They will create a register of people on warfarin and provide user-friendly patient literature describing which other medication to avoid. They intend to standardise their management and improve on the current situation where there is ad hoc follow-up of patients who do not necessarily have their blood checked at the most convenient location or at intended time intervals. The team have searched for examples of good practice and obtained several local and national protocols, and will opt for the arrangement that suits their inner-city setting best. Doctors, nurses and practice managers are cooperating in the initiative and a patient who is on warfarin, is participating in their discussions.

Topics included in this module

- Reducing risks from prescribing
- Good record keeping
- Risk management of clinical conditions
- Health and safety in primary care – risk assessment
- Applying clinical governance to health and safety at work
- Innovation – and risk taking
- Controlling risk factors

Reducing risks from prescribing

All drugs have side effects. Your risk management strategy should be to minimise risks to patients. Your prescribing risk management policy[129–131] should include the following.

- Repeat prescribing protocols for a wide range of different drugs with appropriate time intervals for review. A practice monitoring system should check that defined review intervals are being followed and repeat prescribing systems operating effectively.
- The doctor should initial or countersign any additions or corrections to the prescription.
- Ancillary staff who write or prepare repeat prescriptions should be appropriately trained in the protocols for repeat prescribing, their responsibilities and the need for accuracy.
- Ancillary staff who generate computerised repeat prescriptions should be identifiable via a password for audit purposes.
- Blank prescriptions should never be signed by a doctor for later completion by him/herself or a delegate.
- Unused space should be cancelled out under the last drug on a prescription form.
- Standards set out for the time between receipt of request and production of prescription should allow adequate time for a good-quality repeat prescribing system to operate.
- Written requests for repeat medication are preferable to oral requests – for accuracy, and to reduce opportunities for fraud and misunderstandings.
- General practice prescribing formularies should allow rational prescribing without limiting clinical freedom unduly.
- All repeat prescriptions issued should be noted in the medical records.
- Repeat prescriptions should be discontinued when their therapeutic effect has ceased.
- An efficient repeat prescribing system that eliminates or changes the dose of a specific drug if a doctor stops or changes it, or patients stop taking any repeat prescription.
- 'As required' drugs should be monitored with the same attention as regular medication.
- Repeat prescriptions should not be given more than a few days before the due date.
- Practices should have a standard time limit for the collection of repeat prescriptions (for example seven working days), after which those not collected are destroyed.
- Practices should store repeat prescriptions awaiting collection in a secure way and check that the person collecting the prescription is a trusted representative of the patient.
- Pharmacists should have ready telephone access to GPs to discuss queries about particular prescriptions.
- GPs should learn from outside commentary on their prescribing via systems such as PACT data, feedback from prescribing advisers or community pharmacists.
- GPs should be aware of the potential for fraud at every stage in the repeat prescribing process and set up check systems to monitor that repeat prescriptions are being processed in a reliable way by ancillary staff and medical colleagues.

▼

Good record keeping (*see* Module 4 Reliable and accurate data)

You might test out how you fare against these seven recommended stages in good record keeping that reduce the likelihood of mistakes being made or patient care forgotten.

- **Stage 1**. Are the medical records complete and legible? Have all the health professionals in the practice who are actively contributing to providing care to the patient got access to the medical records and do they consistently write in their reports?
- **Stage 2**. Have the notes been summarised so that the pages are in consecutive order, all the key information is readily available, and any important past and current history has been entered in all the relevant databases and the practice's review systems?

- **Stage 3**. Are the medical records stored in such a way (paper form and/or computerised records) that they can be readily retrieved for use in a consultation. Is the filing up to date so that all correspondence is available when the patient is consulting?
- **Stage 4**. Are all contacts entered in the medical records including telephone consultations?
- **Stage 5**. Are the medical records stored securely in fireproof cabinets if paper-based, with access only to those with authority whether paper-based and/or computer records? Are regular back-ups of computer records made with the back-up disks being stored off the surgery premises?
- **Stage 6**. Are records kept of investigations sent off to check that all results have been received and acted upon?
- **Stage 7**. Do all doctors or the practice as a whole account properly for controlled drugs – new stock received, controlled drugs used and out-of-date stock that is destroyed?

Defence Union records show medication errors are a common cause of claims

196 of 790 claims settled against doctors in a six-year period in the UK were due to medication errors – incorrect or inappropriate drugs, contraindicated medication, administrative error, prescribing or dispensing errors, or prescribing to patients with a known allergy. In 95 of the 196 cases the injury caused was permanent, of which 36 resulted in death, stillbirth or a termination of pregnancy.[132]

Risk management of clinical conditions

You might focus on a significant event such as an unexpected death from an overdose of drugs or an emergency admission for asthma to explore the underlying reasons for that event occurring and to devise new systems to reduce the risk of a similar incident being repeated.

A worked example is given below describing the management of asthma – you can extrapolate the steps to other clinical conditions. Risk management should be targeted at ensuring that:

- new and unknown asthmatics are detected and diagnosed effectively
- patients have ready access to follow-up care and in acute exacerbations
- asthma recall systems work well
- the practice protocol and consequently patient management, adheres to the British Thoracic Society guidelines for asthma care[133]
- practice staff are adequately trained and working within their ability.

Risk management in relation to the care of asthma – an example

1   Establish or update your register of asthmatics – has everyone categorised as having asthma had a reversibility test with bronchodilator drugs at some time? Compare the numbers of asthmatics on your list with the numbers you should expect from national average figures. If too few, should you as a practice be more alert to detecting asthma?

2   Check that everyone in the practice team is familiar with the practice protocol for diagnosing asthmatics and recording in the patients' notes and disease register.

3   Ensure that the practice nurse(s) are adequately trained and working within their ability.

4   Check that your practice protocol matches the British Thoracic Society's guidelines.

5   Look at the equipment in your practice – have you enough peak flow meters and nebulisers and are they functioning? Would a spirometer help to distinguish patients with chronic obstructive airways disease from those with asthma?

6   Review each asthmatic patient's care as they come for follow-up; or call them for a review if they do not present within the time interval laid out in your practice protocol. Check that their self-management plan is adequate, the asthma is not exacerbated by their lifestyle, home or work environment as far as possible, and that their treatment adheres to the British Thoracic Society's guidelines for asthma care.[133]

7   Look at the educational literature you offer patients – could you update it or find something better? Should you write your own text that includes information about the practice's systems and procedures? Does your literature cover all the languages of patients registered with your practice? Do you have non-paper-based patient education materials for those for whom reading is difficult?

8   Audit your care regularly – that follow-up and recall systems are adequate, good inhaler technique, patients use peak flow meters, patients comply with their medication, numbers who continue to smoke and for whom you have recorded their occupation.

9   Obtain patients' feedback about how well your practice systems are working, how convenient your services are, whether education material is appropriate and the service in general. Ask patients for suggestions as to how to improve care and services.

Health and safety in primary care – risk assessment

An employer's duty[134] is to:

- make the workplace safe and without risks to health – of staff or visiting patients
- ensure that articles and substances are moved, stored and used safely
- provide adequate welfare facilities
- inform, instruct, train and supervise staff as necessary for their health and safety
- keep dust, fumes and noise under control
- ensure plant and machinery are safe and that safe systems of work are set and followed

- draw up a health and safety policy statement if there are five or more employees, and make staff aware of the policy and arrangements
- provide adequate first aid facilities.

The extent of risk assessment in general practices

A telephone survey of practice managers and postal study of GPs working in the same 450 general practices in 1997 looked at health at work. The study investigated how many had workplace health policies, and of those with policies how many applied them in practice to manage risks to the health of their staff.[135] The doctors did not always know what policies existed in their practices, leaving that side of the practice operations to their practice managers.

- 87% of practices had a health and safety policy
- 53% carried out risk assessments of health and safety issues
- 42% had carried out a risk reduction programme
- 71% had a policy for the personal safety of staff
- 75% had a system in place in the practice if a member of staff was threatened
- 71% had a sickness absence policy
- 26% had a policy to minimise stress for staff
- 22% had a policy on alcohol and drug misuse in staff

compared with 91% who had a no smoking policy – a much easier policy to draw up than some of the others cited above.

Applying clinical governance to health and safety at work

Examples of how you might do it in bite-sized chunks of work.

- *Confidentiality*: data on staff sickness absence should be kept confidentially, especially if the member of staff is also a patient registered with the practice.
- *Risk management*: anticipate problems by health surveillance looking for common sources of stress for staff; and minimise that stress.
- *Health gain*: safer premises for patients – look for obstacles that might cause patients to trip in the grounds or within the surgery.
- *Health promotion*: assess staff safety and look for ways to improve safety in the surgery and on home visits.
- *Research and development*: is there a burning issue you might investigate such as how practices in your district are sterilising their equipment in main and branch surgeries?

- *Learning culture*: health and safety would be a good topic to discuss as a practice team; you might invite an expert from the health authority on infection control. You could discuss any problems detected by your comprehensive programme on health and safety.
- *Core requirements*: all staff should be aware of the requirement to comply with health and safety law, and the extent to which health and safety laws apply to their posts.
- *Managing resources and services*: branch surgeries should meet the requirements of health and safety laws in just the same way as the main surgery does; equipment must be safe however few patients are using it.
- *Reliable and accurate data*: keep comprehensive records of checks to the sterilising equipment and temperature of fridge storing vaccinations.
- *Involving patients and the public*: ask a patient to walk around the surgery and point out any hazards from the patient's perspective; act on any patients' complaints such as about the examination couch being unstable.
- *Evidence-based practice*: find out and apply best practice in minimising and eliminating cross-infection.
- *Audit*: undertake an audit of manual lifting by staff; if the results are poor in that staff are lifting awkwardly invite a local physiotherapist to give a talk. Review the surgery furniture and storage cabinets to see what improvements you can make.
- *Accountability*: ensure that systems that comply with the law are in place and applied.
- *Coherent teamwork*: check that everyone is up to date with practice systems and procedures for ensuring health and safety.

Innovation – and risk taking

Innovation involves an element of risk taking and uncertainty. The vision of the primary care model of the future with different types of provision will be threatened if the workforce is not sufficiently flexible and willing to adapt to different ways of working. Retention of staff is very important if the innovation is to succeed, for if staff are not supported in change management, a proportion will leave.

There are a number of risks envisaged by those prophesising how primary care will develop – the vision is not without such risks[98] such as:

- the potential loss of the 'personal touch' for patients as some primary care is provided via telephone helplines and information technology
- loss of continuity of care as a trade-off with offering patients more convenient and faster access to primary care advice and information
- insufficient capacity in primary care to meet the expanded range of services envisaged
- staffing, structures and budgets not sufficiently flexible to achieve innovative models of service delivery while retaining uniformly high-quality primary care.

Controlling risk factors

The magnitude of risk is derived from the 'likelihood' and the 'severity' of negative outcomes happening.[136] When people weigh up a risk and make a conscious decision about whether to take that risk they:

- identify the possible options
- identify the consequences or outcomes that might follow from each of those options
- evaluate the desirability of each consequence
- estimate the likelihood of each consequence associated with a specific option
- combine these steps to make a decision – taking into account their own preferences and habitual behaviour.

People usually have a reasonable idea of the *relative risks* of various activities and behaviours, although their estimates of the *magnitude* of risks tend to be biased – small probabilities are often overestimated; and large probabilities are often overestimated. But people may underestimate the risk when they apply relative risks to themselves and their own behaviour – for example, many smokers accept the relationship between smoking tobacco and disease, but do not believe that they are personally at risk.[98] People claim that they are less likely than their peers to suffer harm, which makes it less likely that they take precautions. Thus if you wish to modify people's behaviour so that they adopt less risky lifestyles, you should not only provide information about risk but also reinforce your messages by engaging the person in considering the costs and benefits of the behavioural alternatives.[98]

Relative risk is deduced from comparing the effects of being 'highly' exposed to the risk factor as opposed to being 'slightly' or not at all exposed to that factor. There is a proportional change in the risk of a disease for a given change in the level of the risk factor.

Relative risks[137]

Are often used to compare a population group exposed to a suspected risk with a control group. The ratio of the two incidence rates provides the relative risk of the event occurring in one population group compared to another:

$$\text{Relative risk} = \frac{\text{Incidence rate A}}{\text{Incidence rate B.}}$$

A relative risk close to 1.0 suggests no association between exposure and the outcome (such as a disease).

CardioRisk Manager is a computerised risk assessment package[138,139] that works out a risk calculation for a particular patient according to their blood pressure, cholesterol, smoking status and other relevant factors. It calculates the risk before and after proposed lifestyle changes and additional medication is added to control risk factors. Patients can take home printouts to reinforce the health messages that are essentially engaging them in risk management.

Some ideas on who should do what to put risk management into practice

The GP

- Be clear what employer's responsibilities for health and safety you are delegating to the practice manager.
- Provide resources so that the practice complies with health and safety laws.
- Recognise and anticipate risks and either eliminate, avoid or minimise them.
- Adhere to practice systems and procedures designed to manage risk.

The practice manager

- Establish policies for risk management.
- Monitor policies for risk management.
- Carry out risk reduction programmes in the practice.
- Establish good communication systems in the practice to alert staff about risks.

The practice nurse

- Tend the equipment in the treatment room to minimise risks – ensure that it operates efficiently.
- Store dangerous substances in a secure way.
- Audit attendance at chronic disease management clinics.
- Act if patients default from recall systems and you consider them to be at risk.

The receptionist

- Contribute to any monitoring procedures to detect or review risks.
- Respond to any personal alarm system indicating that a staff member feels threatened.
- Alert doctors and nurses if you pick up signs that patient is at risk, e.g. a severely depressed patient does not return having booked an urgent appointment.

Other attached staff: district nurse, health visitor, community psychiatric nurse, the therapist

- Take personal safety precautions on home visits.
- Adhere to clinical protocols or be able to justify deviation from guidelines.

Action plan: risk management

Today's date: ....   Action plan to be completed by: ....

Tackled by	Identify need/assess problem	Plan of action: what will you do?/by when?
Individual – you		
Practice team – you and your colleagues		
Organisation – your practice		

Evaluation: risk management

Complete as evaluation of progress by ....

Level of evaluation: perspective or work done on this component by	The need or problem	Outcome: what have you achieved?	Who was involved in doing it?	Evaluated: • by whom? • when? • what method was used?
Individual – you				
Practice team – you and your colleagues				
Organisation – your practice				

Record of your learning about 'risk management'

Write in topic, date, time spent, type of learning

	Activity 1	Activity 2	Activity 3	Activity 4
In-house formal learning				
External courses				
Informal and personal				
Qualifications and/or experience gained				

MODULE 13

Accountability and performance

Clinical governance requires all providers of healthcare to have robust and effective systems for ensuring the quality of their services. These should meet national clinical standards. Standards promoted through NSFs or in guidance from NICE should achieve a more uniform quality of care (*see* Module 5 Evidence-based practice and policy).

Local areas may establish their own local accreditation systems. They may produce their own local guidelines and standards or modify national standards or guidance for local circumstances. Local quality monitoring should detect unacceptable variations in performance of practices or practitioners. Those responsible for clinical governance should explore the reasons for substandard performance, offer education and practical support, and require action to rectify shortfalls and improve the quality of healthcare.

Health professionals are accountable to:[140]

- the general public who are entitled to expect high standards of healthcare
- the profession – to maintain standards of knowledge and skills of the profession as a whole
- the government – and employers who expect high standards of healthcare from the workforce.

A recent consultation paper seeks to find ways to identify poor performance at an earlier stage in a systematic way.[141] Regular appraisals are seen as being linked into clinical governance and personal development plans; with referral to an assessment and support service for those whose performance is substandard or who have significant health problems.

Topics included in this module

- Accreditation of healthcare
- Performance assessment framework
- Handling underperformance of clinicians
- Use of performance indicators in general practice
- Core values
- Good medical practice
- Competence
- Quality of care
- Revalidation
- Making decisions about priorities
- Minimising fraud in the NHS

Accreditation of healthcare

Accreditation of healthcare is a 'means of reviewing the quality of the organisation of healthcare using external surveyors and published standards'.[142] It is a system of review using external standards. Accreditation systems are mainly found in the USA, Canada and Australia. Standards may be set nationally and checked locally, or set locally and checked by a national body. The results of accreditation may be confidential to the participating organisation or published to inform the public and purchasers about the performance of local hospitals or health services, especially levels of success and safety.

Accreditation has been directed at the organisation and management of hospitals rather than the clinical competence of doctors and other health professionals. There are moves to incorporate clinical audit and clinical guidelines into accreditation.[143]

The purpose of accreditation is to:[144]

- improve quality – by stimulating changes in practice
- inform decision making – providing information about performance as guidance
- make healthcare organisations accountable to statutory, other agencies or the public
- regulate professional practice and behaviour to protect patients and others.

Accreditation has five key characteristics:[144]

- review of the performance or capacity to perform (e.g. with respect to a hospital, practice or practitioner)
- external involvement of a statutory or professional body and/or peers
- standards to do with aspects of performance or capacity to be assessed and the values or circumstance that are expected
- measurement of performance or capacity to perform against those standards

- report of results – whether performance is at accepted level with recommendations for action.

Accreditation programmes in primary care[144]

- King's Fund Organisational Audit programme – undertaken audits in >250 practices
- Health Services Accreditation programme – has published draft standards for the organisation of primary care and the management of 17 common conditions
- Joint Committee on Postgraduate Training in General Practice (JCPTGP) – training practice assessment; a quarter of UK practices are accredited as training practices
- Royal College of General Practitioners – team-based practice accreditation programme. A local assessment process by the health authority, local medical committee and others
- Royal College of General Practitioners' Fellowship by Assessment scheme
- Royal College of General Practitioners quality practice award

---

Performance assessment framework

There are six components in the NHS performance assessment framework:[145]

- health improvement
- fair access
- efficiency
- effective delivery of appropriate care
- user/carer experience
- health outcomes.

Working through these in the context of assessing the effectiveness of the emergency contraception services for example, might mean that you focus on:

1　Health improvement:
　　– the variability across the district of uptake, e.g. looking at the prescribing data of individual GPs, practices, clinics
　　– whether sexual health promotion given at the same time as emergency contraception is prescribed.
2　Fair access: to all population groups – matched to needs and circumstances. You might look at:
　　– where and when clinics are open
　　– clinic provision compared to other districts.

3   Efficiency:
    –   deployment of doctor–nurse ratio
    –   value for money
4   Effective delivery:
    –   whether given at the right time by most appropriate provider (e.g. available at
        first place of asking such as the A&E department, police station after rape)
    –   good knowledge of availability of providers across district.
5   User/carer experience:
    –   consistency of messages
    –   involvement of parents with those under aged 16 years old.
6   Health outcomes: you might focus on any aspect of the outcomes. For example:
    –   monitor pregnancy rates by age group in district or locality
    –   sexual health matters, e.g. IUCD removals because of infection.

▼
Consistency of messages

Handling underperformance of clinicians

Many health authorities have developed basic screening tools for assessing doctors'
performance to detect significant problems of underperformance. Disentangling the
performance of a practitioner from that of his or her colleagues or working environment,

requires a practice visit to scrutinise the individual's performance, practice management and organisational constraints.

Frequency and nature of serious disciplinary problems among senior medical staff[146]

A report from one region described 96 serious problems that occurred in 49 of 850 hospital specialists over a period of five years. These included:

- poor attitude and disruptive behaviour (32 doctors)
- lack of commitment to duties (21)
- badly exercised clinical skills and inadequate medical knowledge (19)
- dishonesty (11)
- sexual overtones in dealings with patients or staff or both (7)
- disorganised practice and poor communication with colleagues (5).

Twenty five of the 49 doctors retired or left the employer's service; 21 remained in employment after counselling and under supervision.

Guiding principles for dealing with disciplinary problems among doctors[146]

- Remain non-judgemental; beware of manipulation by others with 'axes to grind'
- Be familiar with disciplinary procedures and policies
- Document all matters scrupulously, recording objective evidence
- Confront the problem and sort it out

The action plan for underperformance given in the box below can be applied to health professionals other than GPs. The emphasis is on education and support rather than a punitive approach to underperformance in the first instance; this approach has been endorsed elsewhere.[147]

Action plan for GPs whose performance gives cause for concern in North Staffordshire[148]

- GP Support Panel consisting of representatives from the health authority and local medical committee consider the case and agree there are concerns
- Detailed assessment visit to practice by up to three members of the Support Panel
- Identify and explore concerns with the GP; attempt to diagnose causes of problems
- Agree timed action plan: training needs, facilitate learning, feedback, mentorship
- Support Panel evaluates progress; options are no further action required, ongoing support, further revised action plan and referral to the General Medical Council

Use of performance indicators in general practice

Performance indicators developed by health authorities focus on infrastructure (management, systems, staff time), superstructure (buildings, equipment), educational position (ongoing continuing education) and quality assurance (audit, targets). The focus on structures and procedures is not necessarily related to the quality of clinical care provided, nor does it take into account the patients' perceptions of quality, and variations in provision according to local circumstances and needs.[149]

Indicators commonly used by health authorities in assessing aspects of general practice include:

- numbers of formal complaints (e.g. GPs who have had two or more formal complaints upheld in previous two years)
- standards of medical records: up-to-date summaries
- excessive number of item of service claims compared to peers in locality (e.g. night visits)
- minimal number of item of service claims compared to peers in locality (e.g. contraceptive services)
- prescribing indicators of poor quality of prescribing (e.g. frequent prescribing of benzodiazepines, disproportion of prevention to treatment medication in asthma)[150]
- difficulties of employed staff being released for study leave
- poor immunisation and cervical cytology rates
- failure to apply for postgraduate education allowances (PGEA)
- unjustified requests for removals of patients from GP lists.

There are two approaches to assessing service quality:

- internal review: staff continuously seek ways of improving the quality of care
- external review: independent person or organisation undertakes the assessment, usually measuring standards of the service against externally set standards.

The rigour of external validation may vary from ad hoc surveys and local peer review to involvement in national programmes based on nationally agreed targets for good practice, compliance with which leads to a nationally recognised award. Internal review systems work best when they include monitoring that leads to self-correction where standards slip.

The use of performance indicators by themselves is unlikely to succeed in improving the effectiveness of healthcare in PCGs/PCTs. Evidence-based indicators might improve health outcomes if promoted through educational means,[151] for example:

- aspirin for patients at high risk of coronary or ischaemic cerebrovascular events
- control of hypertension
- advice on stopping smoking

- statins for patients at high risk of coronary heart disease (secondary prevention)
- warfarin for stroke prophylaxis in non-valvular atrial fibrillation.

Core values

An exercise in identifying and rating 'core values' for medical practice in the 21st century confirmed that patient contact and helping individuals were perceived as key factors.[152] The participants of the conference identified and ranked nine core values in the following order:

1 competence
2 caring
3 commitment
4 integrity
5 compassion
6 responsibility
7 confidentiality
8 spirit of enquiry
9 advocacy.

Good medical practice

A recent consultation exercise has described the attributes of an 'excellent' GP and one who is 'unacceptable'. Most of these attributes may be generalised to other health professionals too.

The excellent GP[153]

- takes time to listen to patients and allows them to express their concerns
- includes relevant psychological and social factors as well as physical ones
- uses clear and appropriate language for the patient
- is selective but systematic when examining patients
- performs appropriate skilled examinations with consideration for the patient
- has access to necessary equipment and is skilled in its use
- uses investigations where they will help management
- knows about the nature and reliability of investigations, and understands the results
- makes sound management decisions which are based on good practice and evidence
- maintains his or her knowledge and skills, and is aware of his or her limits of competence

---

The *unacceptable* GP is described as the opposite of most of the above attributes of excellence.

Competence

Responsible clinicians strive to be consciously or unconsciously competent. It is unprofessional to be consciously incompetent or to be unconsciously incompetent where your peers would be expected to have the knowledge and skills to be competent (*see* Figure M13.1).

	Unconscious	*Conscious*
Competence	Unconscious competence	Conscious competence
Incompetence	Unconscious incompetence	Conscious incompetence

Figure M13.1   Competence of clinicians.

A competent clinician will be able to:[154]

* deliver curative and rehabilitative care
* promote health
* organise preventative health-related activities
* plan, organise and evaluate health education activities
* collaborate with other agents of community development
* participate in research and development
* manage his or her services and resources
* learn with, teach and train other members of the healthcare team
* participate in teamwork
* engage in self-directed learning relevant to service needs
* engage in self-evaluation and quality assurance
* be able to demonstrate his or her standards of care and services
* be committed to quality improvement and a clinical governance culture
* involve patients and the public in decision making.

Evidence of competence will include:[155]

* well-defined values, functions, responsibilities and direction
* competent management, good leadership, good systems and data, effective performance monitoring
* consistent, thorough and systematic approach to practice
* evaluation of the impact of care and procedures
* lines of responsibility and accountability clear
* overall performance inspires confidence and trust of patients and the public.

Quality of care

Clinical governance, professional self-regulation and lifelong learning are the three elements that the government envisages being cornerstones in achieving high-quality healthcare[156]. The CHI will help to maintain standards of care through its monitoring function. A broad range of performance indicators should be developed through the NHS Performance Framework to identify indicators that are appropriate for effective monitoring of whether care is of high quality.

The quality of care may be determined by:

- timely access to care
- high-quality clinical care for example diagnosis and clinical management
- high-quality interpersonal care.[157]

The aspects of care that are most highly valued by patients are:[157]

- availability and accessibility of care – appointments, reasonable waiting times, good physical access, ready telephone access
- technical competence – health professional's knowledge and skills, effectiveness of professional's treatment
- communication – time to listen and explain, give information and share in decisions
- interpersonal factors such as health professional being humane, caring, supportive and trustworthy
- good organisation of care – continuity, coordination, near location of services.

Revalidation

The principles of revalidation of professional registration are that the system must:[158]

- be understood by and be credible to the public
- identify unacceptable performance
- identify good performance
- be supported by the profession and must support the profession
- be practical and feasible
- not put any particular group of doctors at an advantage or a disadvantage.

This consultation document recommends that practitioners should be able to submit evidence (which, for minimal additional effort, has been collected for other purposes) to prove that their performance and competence are of an acceptable level.

Making decisions about priorities

In considering the priority to be given to a particular treatment or service, the four dimensions of effectiveness, value, impact and efficiency should be taken into account as well as the public's preferences and views.[159]

- Effectiveness is the extent to which a treatment or other healthcare intervention achieves a desired effect.
- Value is a judgement made by an appropriate group as to how valuable that effect is in one patient relative to the value of other treatments. Quality-adjusted life years (QALYs) are one way of measuring value.
- Impact is the value of an effect weighted for the degree of effectiveness. A treatment or intervention with a high impact will be highly effective and the effect will be considered very valuable by most people (for example extend life by a reasonable amount, good reduction of pain, etc.).
- Efficiency is the cost of the treatment or intervention for a particular level of impact.

There is a wide spectrum in the quality of evidence that is available for different treatments. Evidence for the effectiveness of many treatments or interventions is inconclusive because large, well-designed trials have not been carried out. Such treatments should be distinguished from those for which there is good evidence that they are ineffective. If a low priority were to be given to treatments for which there was no good evidence of effectiveness either way, then we would be biasing the services we commission in favour of ones that are more easily proven.

A local prioritising group at district level or within a PCG or PCT will weigh the evidence for effectiveness, listen to expert perspectives on the alternative treatments and take any biases of the evidence presented into account. The membership of such a group might include representatives from primary care, the local NHS trusts, senior personnel from the health authority such as public health physicians, public representation and the Community Health Council.

Other considerations in the prioritising process will relate to equity of access to the healthcare treatment and patient choice. No particular patient group should be discriminated against, even unintentionally. Follow-up monitoring should check that people receive treatment according to need and that there are no inequities in relation to age, gender, race, religion, location (e.g. rurality, place of abode), beliefs, learning difficulty, lifestyle, employment status or financial status. The prioritising group should include a degree of patient choice when considering what alternative treatments to commission in relation to the expected outcomes of the treatments, the type of interventions and their effects, and expected benefits for the individual concerned.

Minimising fraud in the NHS

Much fraud in the NHS is still thought to be undetected. Prescription fraud alone is estimated to be in excess of £150 million per year in England and Wales.[131] The amount of fraud that was actually detected in the NHS in England and Wales in 1998–99 was £4.7 million, with £3.3 million being in payments for medical services.[160] To put this in context, estimates by the Department of Social Security are of £600 million paid in housing benefits being lost to fraud in the UK each year.[161]

Fraud is legally defined as involving intentional dishonesty and criminal deception rather than sharp practice or ignorance; the person committing fraud knows that they are breaking the law and gains personally from doing so. Preventing fraud is an activity that straddles corporate and clinical governance. Everyone who works in the NHS has a responsibility to use resources effectively and to guard those resources against fraud, whether they are managers, policy makers, clinicians or non-clinical support staff through accountability, probity and openness.

Many of the components of clinical governance will minimise opportunities for fraud in your practice or PCG/PCT. As you improve your systems and procedures to guard against errors or omissions in the delivery of patient care, you automatically make it more difficult for people to perpetrate fraud and not be detected. Evidence-based practice and policy, risk reduction and systematic monitoring, high-quality healthcare with active input from teams of people, and scrutiny from an informed public will all deter fraud or make its detection more likely. High-quality prescribing practices and rational prescribing policies reduce the opportunities for doctors or members of their team to write fraudulent prescriptions or collude with dishonest pharmacists in illegal ways.

Some examples of the scale of fraud in the NHS[162]

- A patient falsely claimed £2500 a year in travel expenses to an outpatient clinic
- A pharmacist and GP conspired together to submit bogus prescriptions for reimbursement of over £1 million
- A dentist falsely claimed £212 000 over two years for patients who did not exist
- Three opticians falsely claimed £25 000 for supplying tinted glasses
- A dispensing GP issued bogus prescriptions for patients in residential homes over three years with a value of more than £700 000
- A GP claimed fees for making 500 night visits in one year against a national average of 50; most of the visits had not been made

---

Some ideas on who should do what about accountability and performance

The GP

- Be accountable for healthcare services in the practice.
- Be accountable for individual patient care.
- Establish methods of proving standards – by a mix of internal and external review.
- Try to live up to the standards of an 'excellent' GP whenever possible.

The practice manager

- Put systems into place that detect or minimise mistakes or fraudulent practices.
- Check that staff are competent to carry out their duties; organise training as necessary.
- Create own performance indicators in practice that link into the PCG/PCT.

The practice nurse

- Cooperate with any monitoring exercise of performance.
- Contribute to assessment of performance by reporting users' experiences.
- Maintain core values to which nursing profession aspires, despite pressure of service commitments.

The receptionist

- Contribute to data collection in any monitoring of systems.
- Adhere to agreed protocols.
- Support doctors and nurses in reaching and sustaining standards of excellence.

Other attached staff: district nurse, health visitor, community psychiatric nurse, the therapist

- Maintain standards when working on own without supervision or observation.
- Keep up to date and maintain competence.

Action plan: accountability and performance

Today's date: ....   Action plan to be completed by: ....

Tackled by	Identify need/assess problem	Plan of action: what will you do?/by when?
Individual – you		
Practice team – you and your colleagues		
Organisation – your practice		

Evaluation: accountability and performance

Complete as evaluation of progress by ....

Level of evaluation: perspective or work done on this component by	The need or problem	Outcome: what have you achieved?	Who was involved in doing it?	Evaluated: • by whom? • when? • what method was used?
Individual – you				
Practice team – you and your colleagues				
Organisation – your practice				

Record of your learning about 'accountability and performance'

Write in topic, date, time spent, type of learning

	Activity 1	Activity 2	Activity 3	Activity 4
In-house formal learning				
External courses				
Informal and personal				
Qualifications and/or experience gained				

MODULE 14

Core requirements

Clinical governance will be a challenge for organisations and staff. It requires a shift in culture, in particular:

- education and training focused on organisational needs and on the needs of the individual
- adequate resources to provide time for the work and for the training
- the identification and development of leaders in every sector
- the development of a non-blaming culture within an organisation.

The NHS Performance Assessment Framework[163] requires health authorities, PCGs and NHS trusts working with social service departments to use the Framework to assess local performance, support the development of the local HImPs and account to ministers and the public for performance by:

- assessing overall performance using the six areas of the framework (*see* Module 13 Accountability and performance)
- comparing service development over time, benchmarking the services with other similar organisations, assessing the reasons for variation and the scope for local improvements, using these comparisons in developing and agreeing local action plans
- incorporating, in future performance and accountability agreements and monitoring arrangements, an assessment of actual and planned progress in the six areas.

The document goes on to say that the local delivery of high-quality healthcare is underpinned by modernised professional self-regulation and extended lifelong learning. With the right staff and the right resources in the right place for the right money, this might be achieved!

Topics included in this module

- Well-trained and competent staff
- Right skill mix
- Safe and comfortable environment
- Cost-effectiveness

Well-trained and competent staff

1   Staff need to be:
    –   correctly qualified to do the job when appointed (*see* Module 2 Managing resources
        and services) or
    –   correctly trained to an assessed competence before working without supervision.
2   Every staff member should have a personal and professional development plan sup-
    ported by management.
3   Identify the education and training needs (not wants) according to:
    –   the requirements of the service
    –   identified individual deficiencies in knowledge skills or attitudes.
4   Education and training should be provided in-house or elsewhere and the time to do
    this supported.

A new minor injuries unit is set up. Two nurses are employed who have already worked on
a similar unit elsewhere. Some of the other nurses who will be working part-time on the unit
need training in assessment and treatment of minor injuries. Their manager releases them
at different times to undergo training at an established unit. A relief nurse is employed to
cover their workload while they are away training.

Review performance continuously by audit to establish competence and identify attitude
problems or gaps in knowledge or skills.

We all need to ensure that team building is not just lots of meetings without a full
interchange of ideas. *See also* Module 8 Coherent teamwork.

The manager arranged for the clerks and clinical staff to meet to iron out problems in the
running of clinics. All the clerks sat together, as did the clinical staff. Two vociferous clinical
staff dominated the discussion of each item and few others were able or willing to express
their opinions. There were many complaints that it was a waste of time.

Risk management is not a blame-and-shame culture. People should feel comfortable
about revealing their own or other peoples' mistakes (*see* Module 12 Risk management).

An abnormal test result had been filed before action. The manager investigating met with
the staff to make a plan to avoid this happening in the future, rather than just censoring the
secretary who had probably placed it in the wrong tray.

We must collect *meaningful* quality measures (*see also* Module 4 Reliable and accurate data).

Crude referral rates are unhelpful. A high rate can conceal gaps in knowledge, skills or resources. Low rates may indicate poor knowledge of secondary facilities or insufficient knowledge of diagnosis. High rates can be due to special interest or demographic peculiarities. Low rates may be due to extensive provision for the condition in primary care.

Right skill mix

People carry out inappropriate tasks because:

* it has always been done that way
* there is no one else to do it
* no one has thought about the best way to do it
* they enjoy doing that job.

Delegation or enhancement

Consider delegation to others who are less expensively paid or less extensively trained. It makes no sense for a doctor to be taking blood samples when a dedicated phlebotomist requires only short-term training and is less expensive. As well as less expensive, the quality of the service may be better, as someone who is concentrating on one task tends to be more skilful. The phlebotomist frees up time for patient care by junior doctors on the wards in hospitals, and by nurses and doctors in general practice settings.

> The development of a practice-based, self-contained community nursing team prompted a reconsideration of how best to make use of the available skill mix. The nursing auxiliary was trained to offer venepuncture to housebound patients to increase the availability of specialised nursing time.

In the UK prior to 1989, two levels of nurse were trained: registered nurses and enrolled nurses. Nurse education moved into higher education and many enrolled nurses converted their qualification to become registered nurses. The introduction of healthcare assistants has followed on from this reduction in skill mix. Concern has been raised that traditional nursing care will be carried out by unqualified or poorly qualified staff as nurses price themselves out of the market.[164]

> A recent study in the UK of nurse practitioners in the accident unit[165] showed that they were assessed as providing as good a service as the junior staff and sometimes better – but at more cost (because of the poor rates of pay of the junior doctors working long hours).

In general practice, trained nurses can successfully provide first contact care for patients with minor illness,[166] take on delegated care from GPs,[167] carry out telephone triage,[168] or run independent new services such as an ear clinic.[169]

In hospitals, nurses increasingly do the jobs that were done by junior hospital doctors – putting up intravenous drips, closure of wounds with stitches and many others. Specialist nurses take on extended roles in many fields traditionally run by doctors. The specialist nurses in epilepsy care, diabetes or neonatal paediatrics are providing liaison services in the community that were done in an inadequate way by hospital-based doctor-led services. The quality of the service is enhanced.

The NHS Executive considers that the new 'nursing role' substitutes for the doctor as doctors' hours are reduced. The widening of nursing skills and the extension of their role puts into doubt their availability to carry out this role in addition to their own.[170] If nurses become more and more qualified and specialised, who will do the basic nursing role?

Nurses taking on responsibilities outside their traditional role must ensure that the tasks are:

- in the patient's best interest
- within their personal skill and competence
- carried out after an enhancement of their knowledge or skills
- not compromising their existing duties
- best carried out by them and not by others with different roles or skills
- and that they are able to be personally accountable for their actions.

It is not just nurses who substitute in traditional professional roles. Anaesthetic technicians, paramedical personnel, pharmaceutical assistants, nursing auxiliaries and many others train to fill specialised roles.

The skill mix included in any team is very wide. Contributions to health authority public health function[171] come from public health physicians, research or information officers, epidemiologists, trainees in public health medicine, nurses, pharmacists, medical advisers and directors of health promotion, among others.

Increasingly, primary care teams are looking for enhancements from other professionals. A pharmacist is likely to add quality to monitoring repeat prescription systems, or reducing duplication of drug or dressing prescriptions.[172] A pharmacist can liaise with nursing homes, reducing expenditure on food supplements and dressings.

A counsellor can take over many of the time-consuming consultations with minor mental illness and distress. Links with the Citizens' Advice Bureau or a social worker who is present in the practice or on the ward round can extend the help available to patients and carers. Voluntary organisations play an important part in supporting and informing patients and carers, especially in conditions where there are gaps in NHS or social service provision or when the condition is uncommon.

Start with finding out what the patients and carers need, then what the service needs, then plan for the people you need to meet those needs – what one paper[173] calls 'reprofiling and aligning skills with organisational needs' for workforce planning.

For other information on skill mix, *see* Module 8 Coherent teamwork.

Safe and comfortable environment

A Health Service Circular[174] reminds us all of good practice in the health, safety and welfare of NHS staff. Managers are responsible for ensuring that they:

- comply with health and safety legislation – there is a lack of knowledge and understanding and compliance can be seriously lacking[175]
- assess risk and where practicable eliminate it
- integrate health and safety with mainstream management (i.e. don't *just* delegate it to a member of staff)
- ensure a partnership between the occupational health service, health and safety management, health promotion services and personnel, and infection control
- set audit standards for the organisation of the service and clinical effectiveness and audit regularly.

Think about risk management in as wide a context as possible. It is not just about avoiding complaints, but also making the working conditions safe and comfortable. Look at Module 2 Managing resources and services. All new staff need an induction pack that includes health and safety recommendations and advice on risk avoidance. This includes the promotion of best practice. Module 5 Evidence-based practice and policy looks at many aspects of good-quality healthcare.

Guidelines on the best practice for the prevention of cross-infection between patients are available. Staff discussion on their practical application should enable them to be put into practice. If practical difficulties are too great, e.g. the unavailability of hand washing facilities, staff need to be able to report the difficulties to someone who can make an action plan to find a remedy for the problems.

An article in 1995[176] found that 85% of general practices in the Liverpool area (74.5% response rate) did not have a written infection control policy. Autoclaves were used in four fifths but most did not have any written procedures for their use. Few practices had any information about procedures for infected patients or staff. A third had no policy on needle-stick injuries, and sharps incidents were recorded in less than half of the surgeries. This prompted training and the development of guidelines focused on the practice nurses.

Staff training should:

- raise awareness about clinical risk management
- include specific training about adverse incident reporting and to whom they should report their concerns

- avoid a blame culture
- include training for those collecting and evaluating data
- show how to promote best practice themselves.

Training and education should work in more than one direction.

A new practice nurse was appointed. She made several suggestions to the practice manager on the running of the treatment room. This streamlined the paperwork and delegated several tasks to unskilled staff, leaving the practice nurse with more time for each patient. Her employing doctors responded by decreasing the allocated time for each nursing appointment. She started looking for another post where she felt her skills would be more appreciated.

Review and control of hazards may include:

- a meeting with the staff concerned to discover the problems
- consideration of staffing levels or skill mix
- training for the work or for avoidance of risk
- developing and implementing protocols and guidelines
- checking building and equipment for suitability and safety
- reporting unsafe practices, equipment or buildings
- seeking expert advice.

A relief nurse found that the workplace sharps container was frequently left on a low table and often filled above the maximum level. She left notes for the regular staff but they were ignored. At a meeting concerning something else, she raised her concerns. An investigation found that the responsibility for sharps boxes had been delegated to a member of staff who was absent on long-term sick leave. Everyone else thought it was someone else's job! Information about the procedure for sharps disposal was disseminated. Each nurse who set up the clinic was given responsibility for renewing and storage of the sharps containers.

Safety is not just safely constructed and maintained buildings and a clear fire exit. The personal safety of staff is extremely important. The design or use of a building can minimise dangerous situations.

A new reception area was planned. The old one had louvres of glass between reception staff and patients. The designer wanted open desks. The staff wanted bullet-proof glass screens on a high counter. After visiting several sites and talking to their staff using open desks, the reception staff agreed to try a high, wide counter with no screens. After installation they were enthusiastic about the reduction in hostility and the increase in their comfort and feeling of security.

Enable staff to have training in recognising the early signs of threat and in how to avoid or defuse confrontations. Help to make them feel more secure by setting up self-defence courses and monitoring of dangerous situations especially if they visit people in their own homes. Provision of a driver for a GP doing a home visit late at night or arranging for a district nurse to take along a colleague makes all the difference to personal comfort with a potentially threatening situation. If the threat is more than suspected, then positive steps such as a police escort or a safer consulting environment with security staff may be required.

> Comfort and good health at work includes the management of mental health and control of excess stress. Common causes of mental distress are lack of control over workload or working standards and lack of appreciation for work well done.

Poor mental health and high stress levels have been reported in staff working in general practice.[135] Sixty five percent of general practitioners felt that stress had caused mistakes in their practices. Other studies have shown similar results for nursing staff, consultants in hospital or staff working in high-dependency residential settings. Support from colleagues and management, time for reflection and discussion as well as avoidance of work overload were all shown to be important factors in preventing burn-out. Look at *Survival Skills for GPs*[177] on how to manage stress levels.

Being safe costs less in the long run.

Cost-effectiveness

Cost-effectiveness is not synonymous with 'cheap'. A cost-effective intervention is one which gives a better or equivalent benefit from the intervention in question for lower or equivalent cost, or where the relative improvement in outcome is higher than the relative difference in cost. In other words, being cost-effective means having the best outcomes for the least input. Using the term 'cost-effective' implies that you have considered potential alternatives.

An intervention must first be considered *clinically* effective to warrant investigation into its potential to be *cost*-effective. Evidence-based practice must incorporate clinical judgement. You have to interpret the evidence when it comes to applying it to individual patients, whether it be evidence about clinical effectiveness or cost-effectiveness.

If you want to ask a question about cost-effectiveness you should be sure to have confirmed clinical effectiveness first, and have gone on to ask a question about cost-effectiveness as the second stage in seeking the evidence. A new or alternative treatment or intervention should be compared directly with the next best treatment or intervention.

An economic evaluation is a comparative analysis of two or more alternatives in terms of their costs and consequences. There are four different types: cost-effectiveness, cost minimisation, cost utility and cost-benefit analyses. Cost-effectiveness analysis is used to compare the effectiveness of two interventions with the same treatment objectives. Cost minimisation compares the costs of alternative treatments which have identical health outcomes. Cost utility analysis enables the effects of alternative interventions to be measured against a combination of life expectancy and quality of life; a common outcome measure being QALYs. A cost-benefit analysis compares the incremental cost and benefits of a programme.

Efficiency is sometimes confused with effectiveness. Being efficient means obtaining the most quality from the least expenditure, or the required level of quality for the least expenditure. To measure efficiency you need to make a judgement about the level of quality of the 'purchase' and be able to relate it to 'price'. 'Price' alone does not measure efficiency. Quality is the indicator used in combination with price to assess if something is more efficient.

So, cost-effectiveness is a measure of efficiency and suggests that costs have been related to effectiveness.

If you have a finite amount of money to spend, it is inescapable that expenditure in one area means less in another. Many NHS staff feel a reluctance to become involved in any financial decision making. They entered the workplace with altruistic motives that did not include having to make difficult decisions about value for money.

Dr M was heard to say at a meeting 'If I wanted to be involved in budgets, I would have gone into business. I just want to be left alone to treat patients'.

Giving people control over their own small budgets and making people aware of the relative costs of treatments can be useful.[178] It gives people the information to take control of how they use supplies, treatments or technologies.

This can be done as a management 'top-down' exercise:

The itemised telephone bill was highlighted to show any items that were questionable. When it was discussed at the staff meeting, it provoked suggestions and changes in the use of the phone. Staff reminded each other about the direct line access and began to put helpful messages next to phone numbers about who and when to call. Reductions in outgoing calls enabled more incoming telephone consultations and a saving in time as well as costs.

Or as an initiative from a clinical group or team:

The treatment room nurses looked at the cost of gloves. They found that placing boxes of cheaper utility gloves next to cleaning sinks prevented the use of the more expensive surgical gloves and reduced costs.

Not all measures are to contain costs. You may need to spend more in one area to provide interventions to maximise health gain. Innovations in treatments and technologies have to be evaluated for effectiveness and compared with established ones for economic value.

Considerable uncertainty exists in trying to work out how to compare interventions in terms of the extra cost per unit of health outcome obtained, because:

- health economists are still debating the methodological framework underlying the decisions
- the data are uncertain because:
  - assumptions are made in different ways
  - data are missing
  - the data are interpreted in different ways
- the presentation and interpretation of the results are often subjective or biased.

Reading the letters in response to articles proposing one course of action over another reveals many biases and the subjective reasoning involved. Both the correspondents and the authors of the original articles can become quite heated in their defence of their own point of view. Unless the argument is completely overwhelming and supported by irrefutable evidence in favour of one view, it is easy to be swayed first one way and then another by the arguments.

There is considerable scope for improving existing methods. Types of costs involved in studies of cost-effectiveness include the following:

Health service costs	Non-health service costs	Other costs
Costs of the study	Costs incurred in other public sector budgets such as social services	Transfer costs where money flows from one group in society to another (e.g. from taxes to social security payments)
Direct costs of the intervention	Informal care costs	
Costs of treating other illnesses arising from the intervention	Patients' travel costs	
Costs of treating other unrelated illnesses discovered during the intervention study	Other out-of-pocket expenses incurred by the patients	
Future costs incurred because of any lengthening of life resulting from the intervention	Patients' time costs taken up by the intervention	
	Productivity and work time costs taken up by the intervention	
	Future costs incurred because of any lengthening of life resulting from the intervention	

How value is put on health is even more difficult to quantify. Measures of health-related quality of life (HRQoL) are used to generate QALYs.[179]

Even if they are valid in a descriptive sense, these measures may not be suitable for economic evaluation.

Techniques for eliciting values for health include:

- *Visual analogue scale*, for example:
  [Most preferred health state] ——————————————— [least preferred health state]
- *Magnitude estimation*, for example:
  Is [state A] two times worse than [state B] or three times worse, etc.?
- *Standard gamble*, for example:
  Balancing [years of life gained] against [quality of life gained] for a procedure or treatment.
- *Time trade-off*, for example:
  [Increased life expectancy with a chronic condition followed by death] traded off against [health restored for a shorter time followed by death].

Think about introducing three stages in managing cost-effectiveness evaluations:

1   Identify new healthcare interventions *before* they become established.[180]

> The introduction of laparoscopic surgery in the early 1990s was referred to as 'the biggest unaudited free-for-all in the history of surgery'.

2   Decide on the optimum time to evaluate a new intervention.

> Laparoscopic surgery was evaluated too late; expectations had already been created.

3   After evaluation, improve on the implementation of any research finding.

It is not clear how best to do this. It appears that a combination of audit and feedback works better than most methods. Computer-generated reminders work for some things. Have a look at a review of the studies published so far.[181]

> Evaluations of telemedicine are continuing; fortunately the slow introduction of this tool is allowing a measured approach. It is a low-risk innovation, but if a serious misdiagnosis occurred a rapid increase in evaluative studies would be demanded.

It takes time to implement research findings.

> Two years after the publication of evidence to show that norethisterone did not reduce heavy periods and that tranexamic acid or non-steroidal antinflammatory drugs were preferable, most patients were still being prescribed norethisterone.

Using treatments that do not work, even if they are inexpensive, is a waste of money and resources. Using expensive treatments that work marginally better than less expensive (but almost as effective) treatments may not be best value for money.

Some ideas on who should do what to strengthen core requirements

Many of the core requirements will be covered by activities in other modules.

The GP

- Be proactive about changing skill mix.
- Be responsible for monitoring cost-effective information.
- Monitor outcomes of care.
- Link practice up with occupational health scheme.

The practice manager

- Establish clear lines of accountability.
- Take overall responsibility for employing well-trained and competent staff.
- Support staff.
- Be responsible for safety and comfort of staff.

The practice nurse

- Pursue reflective practice around skill mix.
- Feed back to others on patient and carer experience.

The receptionist

- Report safety hazards.
- Relay feedback from patients.
- Ensure fair access to health professionals and services.

Other attached staff: district nurse, health visitor, community psychiatric nurse, the therapist

- Relay feedback from users, carers, the public.
- Adopt flexible working to provide the right skill mix.
- Maintain competence and professional standards.

Action plan: core requirements

Today's date: ....   Action plan to be completed by: ....

Tackled by	Identify need/assess problem	Plan of action: what will you do?/by when?
Individual – you		
Practice team – you and your colleagues		
Organisation – your practice		

Evaluation: core requirements

Complete as evaluation of progress by ....

Level of evaluation: perspective or work done on this component by	The need or problem	Outcome: what have you achieved?	Who was involved in doing it?	Evaluated: • by whom? • when? • what method was used?
Individual – you				
Practice team – you and your colleagues				
Organisation – your practice				

Record of your learning about 'core requirements'

Write in topic, date, time spent, type of learning

	Activity 1	Activity 2	Activity 3	Activity 4
In-house formal learning				
External courses				
Informal and personal				
Qualifications and/or experience gained				

Quality improvement

Challenges of quality improvement

Clinical governance is a new name for joining together many things that we already do to a greater or lesser degree. It is a framework for the improvement of patient care through achieving high standards, reflective practice and risk management as well as personal and professional development. The enhancement of quality of care is based on each and every module in this book.

The challenges of definition

'Quality' is a key word in any statements about clinical governance but there are many definitions of the word. If you look in a dictionary the word means:

- a characteristic or attribute of something; a property; a feature
- the natural or essential character of something
- the degree or grade of excellence
- excellence or superiority.

Roy Lilley[1] defines it as:

> 'Knowing what outcome you want and being sure you get it, every time, for as long as you want it'

The needs and expectations of the user will alter the precise definition of quality. The service provided must fit the needs of the user within the constraints of cost and present levels of knowledge and technology. The priority is to understand the needs of the users and then, and only then, to provide for these. Everyone involved in the delivery of healthcare should work cooperatively and in a complementary way. We have to develop methods to measure how well the need is met in order to monitor and then improve the service.

If the service is developed to meet the needs of those supplying it (as has been done all too often in the past), bias creeps in. If a service is modified without considering all the ramifications of the change, control over resources may be shifted without real benefit.

A GP had two patients who both needed to see the specialist. The patients complained about the difficulties of travel to the hospital and the GP had the bright idea of pleasing his patients by asking the specialist to see patients in his surgery. The specialist was delighted at first – flattered to be asked and pleased to be out of the rush of outpatients to see a few patients in comfortable surroundings. The hospital manager was horrified – not cost-effective to see so few patients and the specialist was out of the hospital for half a day. The specialist became disenchanted. There was more pressure on his remaining outpatient clinics; he had no junior staff at the outreach clinic to screen out the boring patients, no nurses running around making sure everything was done. If anyone had consulted the two patients who started it all, they might have found out that it was all a waste of effort. They had to attend the hospital anyway for tests and they had doubts about whether a chap seen in their doctor's surgery was a proper specialist!

All of those involved in the delivery of care tend to emphasise the value of the particular parts of the care process central to their particular role. Surgeons concentrate on the importance of access to operations but anaesthetists focus on the availability of intensive care beds. The physician puts more emphasis on drug therapy (and so do pharmaceutical companies) but the physiotherapist wants more equipment. Doctors want to make people well again but nurses see their role as helping people to cope with the illness better. Social workers have their eyes fixed on the coping and caring mechanisms, never mind the illness. Service managers look at cost containment and public health doctors at cost effectiveness.

If quality is defined in partial terms, separating out any of these aspects from another will give priority to one particular view – and it may not be the one that improves the quality of care for the patient.

To reduce bias, use a comprehensive multidimensional model based on the Donebedian one (*see* Module 9 Audit and evaluation) in the table opposite.

Challenges of measurement

Those facets of the health service that are easiest to quantify are not always the most important.[182] Patients often put more value on 'He's such a caring person' than 'He's always going on courses to keep up to date'. Managers often make sure that those things that can be measured are done (targets for health promotion) rather than those things that are difficult to measure (visiting a dying patient).

There is no reason why qualitative measures[183] should not be used alongside quantitative ones. Failures in the past to appreciate the importance of using appropriate measurements have acted as barriers to improvements. League tables and other simplistic measures distort needs and the delivery of care.

	Structure (resources)	Process (activities)	Outcome (results)
Effectiveness	Do staff qualifications conform with stated requirements?	Are best practice guidelines and protocols adhered to?	
Acceptability	To what extent are the facilities judged satisfactory by users?		Is the quality of life available to sufferers acceptable to them and to the community?
Efficiency			How does the cost per successful unit of treatment compare in one provider unit as opposed to another?
Access		What proportion of the total population in need of treatment receives it, after how long?	
Equity		Is there bias in access between social groups, and is this judged fair by the community?	
Relevance	Do staff deployments match the patterns of expressed consumer need?		Do health gains resulting from existing patterns of care match those that could be generated by alternatives?

Challenges of where and how to deliver care

Health and social care can be analysed at three distinct levels:

1   At the community level, involving care for the whole population. Taxation or insurance schemes fund equitable levels of care for all. The system is run through official bureaucracy and is politically based.
2   At the institutional or managerial level, by a particular hospital or practice serving part of a population. The user or their agent makes the choice of the particular unit or service provided.
3   At the individual or professional level, focused on the interests of particular patients. It is driven by peer-group pressure, ethics and moral values.

Much of health promotion activity has to be done at the first, political level (*see* Module 11 Health promotion) and resources can be directed to particular areas for clinical care. Efficiency of care and service improvements typically have occurred at level two, and clinical effectiveness and personal care at level three.

Delivery of quality care has been marked by conflicts between these levels. We need to find effective ways of working cooperatively to produce quality improvements.

The challenge of how to deal with poor quality

Too many managers and bosses still believe that fear of punishment is the only way to get things done. All the evidence suggests that this produces defensiveness and concealment of difficulties and errors. The logic of management requires attitudes that support rather than punish (*see* Module 2 Managing resources and services) and recognising that most people wish to work well and assist those around them.

There is a real fear that audit, evaluation, reaccreditation or any other part of clinical governance will be used as a stick to beat the workers. Of course, there will be some who do produce poor results and even fewer who cannot be helped to improve. Mechanisms to cope with this group must be thought out carefully, while celebrating success and supporting the development of the rest.

The challenge of who is the health service for?

There is a real danger that we will lose sight of the patients, users and public. It often seemed that, at one time, the health service was run for the teaching hospital consultants. Then the managers, many of whom were from non-medical backgrounds, supplanted them. Now the PCGs are largely chaired by GPs and have a preponderance of doctors. We will have to guard against accusations of top-down management by real consultation of service users (*see* Module 10 Meaningful patient and public involvement).

Valuing patients and staff, making them partners, giving them responsibility for their own work and health, all help to make the transition to a better quality of care.

Challenges of resources

Very little has been offered to support clinical governance. It may be integral to our daily work, but it does not come without investment in time and costs. It is fallacious to suggest that clinical governance will result in overall savings or cost. Quality does not come free. Development cannot be done if there is no extra money. Money saved by reducing or cutting an ineffective service will be more than countered by the upsurge in demand and expectations from a closer attention to the needs of the users for a good-quality service.

The challenge across the country

We have all heard or seen examples of excellence in healthcare. Our challenge is to move from:

establishing minimum reasonable standards for care

to

identifying customary standards

and then to

recommended best practice.

Appendix: resources

Useful worldwide web addresses

ARIF (Aggressive Research Intelligence Facility): http://www.org.uk/links/arif/arifhome.htm The University of Birmingham, 27 Highfield Road, Edgbaston, Birmingham B15 3DP.

Bandolier: http://www.jr2.ox.ac.uk/bandolier/index.html

CASP (Critical Appraisal Skills Project) http://www.his.ox.ac.uk/casp

CEBM (Centre for Evidence-Based Medicine): http://cebm.jr2.ox.ac.uk/

Clinical Evidence from the British Medical Journal Publishing Group. An electronic version will be available in 2000. See http://www.evidence.org

The Cochrane Library, Update Software, Summertown Pavilion, Middle Way, Summertown, Oxford OX2 7LG. http://www.cochrane.co.uk or http://www.doctors.net.uk (GMC registration number required).

DARE (Database of Abstracts of Reviews of Effectiveness) contains high-quality research reviews of the effectiveness of healthcare interventions: http://nhscrd.york.ac.uk/welcome.html

Guidelines database containing a summary, a detailed critical appraisal about the quality and robustness, and a link to the detailed document: http://www.his.ox.ac.uk/guidelines/

Healthfinder: http://www.healthfinder.org/

Medical Matrix: http://www.medmatrix.org/index.stm

Medline: http://www.ncbi.nlm.nih.gov/PubMed

OMNI: http://www.omni.ac.uk

PuBMed National Library of Medicine search service to access MEDLINE with links to allied journals: http://www4.ncbi.nlm.gov/PubMed

REHABDATA is a bibliographic database for rehabilitation, disability and assistive technology: http://207.252.36.100/naric.htm

ScHaRR Introduction to Free Databases: http://www.shef.ac.uk/~scharr/ir/trawling.html

STATS (Steve's Attempt To Teach Statistics): http://www.cmh.edu/stats

WISDOM (part of the Institute of General Practice and Primary Care, University of Sheffield): http://www.wisdom.org.uk

Useful publications on evidence-based practice and clinical effectiveness

Bandolier is published by the NHS Executive, Anglia and Oxford, as a monthly newsletter that describes the literature on the effectiveness of healthcare interventions in a pithy style. Moore A, McQuay H (eds) Bandolier, Pain Relief Unit, The Churchill, Oxford OX3 7LJ. http://www.jr2.ox.ac.uk/Bandolier

Clinical Evidence A twice-yearly compendium of the best available evidence for effective healthcare. BMJ Publishing Group. Launched in 1999.

Clinical Effectiveness Resource Pack This resource pack is updated regularly and is produced by the NHS Executive. It includes lists of contact details for many organisations, publications and other sources of information on clinical effectiveness. There is also information about associated publications – the Effective Health Care Bulletins, Effectiveness Matters, Epidemiologically Based Needs Assessments, Systematic Reviews of Research Evidence, Clinical Guidelines, Health Technology Assessments and other relevant publications.

Effective Healthcare Bulletins These bulletins are produced by the NHS Centre for Reviews and Dissemination at the University of York. They are 'based on systematic review and synthesis of research on the clinical effectiveness, cost-effectiveness and acceptability of health service interventions'. NHS Centre for Reviews and Dissemination, University of York, York YO1 5DD. Subscriptions and copies from Royal Society of Medicine Press, PO Box 9002, London W1A OZA.

He@lth Information on the Internet This is a bimonthly newsletter for all healthcare professionals published by The Royal Society of Medicine in association with the Wellcome Trust. He@lth Information on the Internet published by The Royal Society of Medicine, 1 Wimpole Street, London W1M 8AE. Tel 020 7290 2927.

Health Updates from the Health Education Authority. Topics in the series are: Coronary Heart Disease, Smoking, Alcohol, Physical Activity, Workplace Health, Child Health, Immunisation. These are well-researched reference books on topical health issues. Health Education Authority; Health Update; Health Education Authority, Trevelyan House, 30 Great Peter Street, London SW1P 2HW.

Woodrow P (1996) Exploring confidentiality in nursing practice. *Nursing Standard.* **10**: 38–42.

Relevant books

Armstrong R and Grace J (1994) *Research Methods and Audit in General Practice.* Oxford University Press, Oxford.

Baker M, Maskrey N and Kirk S (1997) *Clinical Effectiveness and Primary Care.* Radcliffe Medical Press, Oxford.

BMA Handbook Working Party (1998) *Philosophy and Practice of Medical Ethics.* British Medical Association, London.

Carter Y and Thomas C (eds) (1997) *Research Methods in Primary Care.* Radcliffe Medical Press, Oxford.

Chambers R (1998) *Clinical Effectiveness Made Easy.* Radcliffe Medical Press, Oxford.

Chambers R (1999) *Involving Patients and the Public: how to do it better.* Radcliffe Medical Press, Oxford.

Chambers R, Hawksley B and Teeranlall R (1999) *Survival Skills for Nurses.* Radcliffe Medical Press, Oxford.

Chambers R and Wall D (2000) *Teaching Made Easy: a manual for health professionals.* Radcliffe Medical Press, Oxford.

Crombie I (1996) *The Pocket Guide to Critical Appraisal.* BMJ Publishing Group, London.

Deighan M and Hitch S (eds) (1999) *Clinical Effectiveness from Guidelines to Cost-effective Practice.* Earlybrave, Brentwood.

Elwyn G and Smail J (1999) *Integrated Teams in Primary Care.* Radcliffe Medical Press, Oxford.

Gillies A (1999) *Information and IT for Primary Care.* Radcliffe Medical Press, Oxford.

Gray JAM (1997) *Evidence-based Healthcare.* Churchill Livingstone, Edinburgh.

Greenhalgh T (1997) *How to Read a Paper: the basics of evidence-based medicine.* BMJ Publishing Group, London.

Jones R and Kinmonth AL (eds) (1999) *Critical Reading for Primary Care.* Oxford University Press, London.

Jones R and Menzies S (1999) *General Practice: Essential Facts.* Radcliffe Medical Press, Oxford.

Kiley R (1999) *Medical Information on the Internet* (2e). Harcourt Publishers, London (includes free CD-ROM).

King's Fund (1998) *Turning Evidence into Everyday Practice*. King's Fund, London.

Kobelt G (1996) *Health Economics: An introduction to economic evaluation*. Office of Health Economics, London.

Lancaster T, Strauss S, Badenoch D, Richardson S *et al.* (1998) *Practising Evidence-based Medicine*. Learner's manual (3e). Radcliffe Medical Press, Oxford.

Ling T (ed) (1999) *Reforming Healthcare by Consent*. Radcliffe Medical Press, Oxford.

Li Wan Po A (1998) *Dictionary of Evidence-based Medicine*. Radcliffe Medical Press, Oxford.

Lugon M and Secker-Walker J (1999) *Clinical Governance: making it happen*. Royal Society of Medicine Press, London.

NHS Executive (1996) *Patient Partnership: building a collaborative strategy*. Department of Health, Leeds.

Pike S and Forster D (1995) *Health Promotion for All*. Churchill Livingstone, Edinburgh. (This book contains a framework for developing a personal health promotion portfolio.)

Sackett D, Richardson S, Rosenberg W and Haynes RB (1997) *Evidence-based Medicine*. Churchill Livingstone, Edinburgh.

Strauss S, Badenoch D, Richardson S *et al.* (1998) *Practising Evidence-based Medicine*. Tutor's Manual (3e). Radcliffe Medical Press, Oxford.

Tyrrell S (1999) *Using the Internet in Healthcare*. Radcliffe Medical Press, Oxford.

van Zwanenberg T and Harrison J (eds) (2000) *Clinical Governance in Primary Care*. Radcliffe Medical Press, Oxford.

Wilson T (1999) *The PCG Development Guide*. Radcliffe Medical Press, Oxford.

References

1   Lilley R (1999) *Making Sense of Clinical Governance*. Radcliffe Medical Press, Oxford.

2   Chambers R and Wall D (1999) *Teaching Made Easy: a manual for health professionals*. Radcliffe Medical Press, Oxford.

3   Department of Health (1998) *A First Class Service: quality in the new NHS*. Health Service Circular HSC 1998/113. Department of Health, London.

4   Department of Health (1997) *The New NHS: modern, dependable*. The Stationery Office, London.

5   Scally G and Donaldson IJ (1998) Clinical governance and the drive for quality improvement in the new NHS in England. *BMJ*. **317**: 61–5.

6   Goodman N (2000) Accountability, clinical governance and the acceptance of imperfection. *J Roy Soc Med*. **93**: 56–8.

7   Greenhalgh T (1997) *How to Read a Paper*. BMJ Publishing, London.

8   Department of Health (1999) *Clinical Governance: quality in the new NHS*. Health Service Circular HSC (99) 065. Department of Health, London.

9   van Zwanenberg T and Harrison J (2000) *Clinical Governance in Primary Care*. Radcliffe Medical Press, Oxford.

10 Mulley A (1999) Learning from differences within the NHS. *BMJ*. **319**: 528–30.

11 Chief Nursing Officer (1998) *Integrating Theory and Practice in Nursing*. NHS Executive, London.

12 Macleod N, Moloney R and Chambers R (1999) *The Education and Training Needs of Primary Care Groups: supporting staff to meet the needs*. Staffordshire University, Stoke-on-Trent.

13 Wilson T, Butler F and Watson M (1998) Establishing educational needs in a new organisation. *Career Focus, BMJ*. **317**: 2–3.

14 Seagraves L, Osborne N, Neal P *et al.* (1996) *Learning in Smaller Companies (LISC) Final Report*. University of Stirling, Stirling.

15 Chambers R and Schrijver E (1999) *Making Practice-based Professional Development Plans Relevant to Service Needs and Priorities*. Staffordshire University, Stoke-on-Trent (submitted for publication).

16 Feather A and Fry H (1999) Key aspects of teaching and learning in medicine and dentistry. In: Fry H, Ketteridge S and Marshall S (eds) *A Handbook for Teaching and Learning in Higher Education*. Kogan Page, London.

17 National Health Service Executive (1998) *Working Together: securing a quality workforce for the NHS*. Department of Health, London.

18 Roland M, Holden J and Campbell S (1999) *Quality Assessment for General Practice: supporting clinical governance in primary care groups*. National Primary Care Research and Development Centre, University of Manchester, Manchester.

19 Standing Committee on Postgraduate Medical and Dental Education (1997) *Multi-professional Working and Learning: sharing the educational challenge.* SCOPME, London.

20 Miller C, Ross N and Freeman M (1999) *Researching Professional Education.* Research reports series No 14. English National Board for Nursing, Midwifery and Health Visiting, Cambridge.

21 Calman K (1998) *A Review of Continuing Professional Development in General Practice.* Chief Medical Officer, Department of Health, London.

22 Standing Committee on Postgraduate Medical and Dental Education (1998) *Continuing Professional Development for Doctors and Dentists.* SCOPME, London.

23 Chambers R (1998) *Clinical Effectiveness Made Easy.* Radcliffe Medical Press, Oxford.

24 Elwyn G and Smail J (1999) *Integrated Teams in Primary Care.* Radcliffe Medical Press, Oxford.

25 Chambers R (1999) *Involving Patients and the Public.* Radcliffe Medical Press, Oxford.

26 Sanderson H (ed) (1998) *Casemix for All.* Radcliffe Medical Press, Oxford.

27 Lilley R (1999) *Writing Investment Plans and Health Improvement Programmes.* Radcliffe Medical Press, Oxford.

28 Riley J (1998) *Helping Doctors Who Manage.* King's Fund Publishing, London.

29 Mullen P and Spurgeon P (1999) *Priority Setting and The Public.* Radcliffe Medical Press, Oxford.

30 Benson T and Neame R (1994) *Healthcare Computing.* Longman Group, Harlow.

31 Mant D (1997) *R and D in Primary Care.* NHS Executive, Wetherby.

32 NHS Executive (1998) *Research: what's in it for consumers?* NHS Executive, Wetherby.

33 Morrison J, Sullivan F, Murray E and Jolly B (1999) Evidence-based education: development of an instrument to critically appraise reports of educational interventions. *Medical Education.* **33**: 890–3.

34 National Primary Care Research and Development Centre, University of Manchester. www.npcrdc.man.ac.uk

35 Griffith SM, Kaira D, Lloyd D, Grubb P *et al.* (1995) A portable communicative architecture for electronic healthcare records: the good European health record project. *Medinfo.* **8** (1): 223–36.

36 Neame R (1997) Smart cards – the key to trustworthy health information systems. *BMJ.* **314**: 573–7.

37 Godlee F (ed) (updated every six months) *Clinical Evidence.* BMJ Publishing Group, London.

38 Coulter A (1998) Evidence based patient information is important, so there needs to be a national strategy to ensure it. *BMJ.* **317**: 225–6.

39 Wyatt JC (1997) Commentary: measuring quality and impact of the World Wide Web. *BMJ.* **314**: 1879–81.

40 http://www.discern.org.uk

41 http://www.hfht.org.chiq

42 Watts LA and Monk AF (1999) Tele-medicine. What happens in remote consultations. *International Journal Technological Assessment Health Care.* **15**: 220–35.

43 Charles R (1994) An evaluation of parent-held child health records. *Health Visitor.* **67**: 270–2.

44 Kirkham M (1997) Client held notes: talisman or truly shared resource. *Modern Midwife.* **7**: 15–17.

45 Ayana M, Pound P and Ebrahim S (1998) The views of therapists on the use of a patient-held record in the care of stroke patients. *Clinical Rehabilitation.* **12**: 328–37.

46 Baker J (1996) Shared record keeping in the multidisciplinary team. *Nursing Standard.* **10**: 39–41.

47 NHS Executive (1996) *Promoting Clinical Effectiveness.* NHS Executive, London.

48 Sackett DL, Rosenberg WM, Gray J *et al.* (1996) Evidence-based medicine: what it is, and what it isn't. *BMJ.* **312**: 71–2.

49 The King's Fund (1997) *Turning Evidence Into Everyday Practice.* The King's Fund, London.

50 Carter Y and Falshaw M (eds) (1998) *Introduction to Evidence-based Primary Care and its Application in Commissioning.* An open learning programme, *Evidence-based Primary Care.* Radcliffe Medical Press, Oxford.

51 NHS Centre for Reviews and Dissemination (1999) Getting evidence into practice. *Effective Health Care Bulletin.* **5**(1). Royal Society of Medicine Press, London.

52 Harlow T (1999) BHS guidelines simplify GP management of hypertension. *Guidelines in Practice.* **2 December**: 31–5.

53 Ramsay LE, Williams B, Johnston GD *et al.* (1999) British Hypertension Society guidelines for hypertension management 1999: summary. *BMJ.* **319**: 630–5.

54 Carter Y and Falshaw M (eds) (1998) *Finding the Papers: a guide to Medline searching.* An open learning programme, *Evidence-based Primary Care.* Radcliffe Medical Press, Oxford.

55 Nagle J and Streiffer R (1996) *Evidence-based patient education. What really works?* Paper presented at Patient Education Conference, Nashville.

56 Donaldson K (ed) (1999) *Public and Professional Partnerships in Clinical Effectiveness.* Report of Conference, Scottish, Clinical Resource and Audit Group (CRAG), Edinburgh.

57 Eysenbach G and Diepgen T (1999) Patients looking for information on the Internet and seeking teleadvice. *Arch Dermatol.* **135**: 151–6.

58 Kaplan SH, Greenfield S and Ware JE (1989) Assessing the effects of physician–patient interactions on the outcomes of chronic disease. *Med Care.* S110–27.

59 Hall JA, Roter DL and Katz NR (1988) Meta-analysis of correlates of provider behavior in medical encounters. *Med Care.* **26**(7): 657–75.

60 Kaplan SH, Gandek B, Greenfield S *et al.* (1995) Patients' and visit characteristics related to physicians' participatory decision-making style. *Med Care.* **33**(12): 1176–87.

61 Miller C, Ross N and Freeman M (1999) *Shared Learning and Clinical Teamwork: new directions in education for multi-professional practice.* English National Board for Nursing, Midwifery and Health Visiting, London.

62 Department of Health (1999) *National Service Framework for Mental Health.* NHS Executive, London. www.doh.gov.uk/nsf/mentalhealth.htm

63 Smith P (ed) (1997) *Guide to the Guidelines: disease management made simple* (3e). Radcliffe Medical Press, Oxford.

64 Carman D and Britten N (1995) Confidentiality of medical records: the patients' perspective. *Br J Gen Pract.* **45**: 485–8.

65 Allen I (1991) *Family Planning and Pregnancy Counselling for Young People.* Policy Studies Institute, London.

66 Howell M (1994) Confidentiality during staff reports at the bedside. *Nursing Times.* **90**: 44–5.

67 Woodrow P (1996) Exploring confidentiality in nursing practice. *Nursing Standard.* **10**: 38–42.

68 Glen S (1997) Confidentiality: a critique of the traditional view. *Nursing Ethics.* **4**: 403–6.

69 Department of Health (1997) *Report of the Review of Patient-identifiable Information* (The Caldicott Committee report). Department of Health, London.

70 Fisher F and Madge B (1996) Data security and patient confidentiality. *International Journal of Biomedical Computing.* **43**: 115–19.

71 Genesen L *et al.* (1994) Faxing medical records: another threat to confidentiality in medicine. *JAMA.* **271**: 1401–2.

72 Lorge RE (1989) How informed is patient's consent to the release of medical information to insurance companies? *BMJ.* **298**: 1495–6.

73 Jacobson B, Smith A and Whitehead M (1991) *The Nation's Health: a strategy for the 1990s.* King Edward's Hospital Fund for London, London.

74 Forrest Sir Patrick (chair) (1986) *Breast Cancer Screening.* Report to the health ministers of England, Wales, Scotland and Northern Ireland. HMSO, London.

75 Black Sir Douglas (chair) (1980) *Inequalities in Health.* Report of a research working group. Department of Health & Social Security, London.

76 Whitehead M (1988) The health divide. In: *Inequalities in Health.* Penguin, London.

77 Wigersma L and Oud R (1987) Safety and acceptability of condoms for use by homosexual men against transmission of HIV during anogenital sexual intercourse. *BMJ.* **295**: 11.

78 Nardone A, Mercey DE and Johnson AM (1997) Surveillance of sexual behaviour among homosexual men in a central London health authority. *Genitourinary Medicine.* **73**: 198–202.

79 Taylor D (1998) *Improving Health Care.* King's Fund Publishing, London.

80 Botvin GJ, Baker E, Dusenbury L, Botvin EM and Diaz T (1995) Long-term follow-up of a randomized drug abuse prevention trial in a white middle-class population. *JAMA.* **273**: 1106–12.

81 Lancaster T, Silagy C, Fowler G and Spiers I (1999) Training health professionals in smoking cessation. In: *The Cochrane Library.* Update Software, Oxford.

82 Wilson JMG (1976) Some principles of early diagnosis and detection. In: Teeling-Smith G (ed) *Proceedings of a Colloquium, Magdalen College, Oxford.* Office of Health Economics, London.

83 Clarke R and Croft P (1998) *Critical Reading for the Reflective Practitioner.* Butterworth-Heinemann, Oxford.

84   Wilkinson CE, Jones JM and McBride J (1990) Anxiety caused by abnormal results of a cervical smear test: a controlled trial. *BMJ.* **300**: 440.

85   Wilkinson C (1992) Abnormal cervical smear test results: old dilemmas and new directions. *Br J Gen Pract.* **42**: 336–9.

86   Griffin S and Kinmonth AL (1997) Diabetes Care: the effectiveness of systems for routine surveillance for people with diabetes (Cochrane Review). In: *The Cochrane Library.* Update Software, Oxford.

87   Charlton I *et al.* (1991) Audit of the effect of a nurse run asthma clinic on workload and patient morbidity in a general practice. *Br J Gen Pract.* **41**: 227–31.

88   Keeley D (1993) How to achieve better outcome in the treatment of asthma in general practice. *BMJ.* **307**: 1261–3.

89   Robertson R, Osman LM and Douglas JG (1997) Adult asthma review in general practice: nurses' perception of their role. *Family Practice.* **14**: 227–32.

90   Antiplatelet trialist collaborations (1994) Collaborative overview of randomised trials of antiplatelet therapy: prevention of deaths, myocardial infarction and stroke by prolonged antiplatelet therapy in various categories of patients. *BMJ.* **308**: 81–106.

91   Gould ANL *et al.* (1998) Cholesterol reduction yields clinical benefit: impact of statin trials. *Circulation.* **97**: 9462–520.

92   Yusuf S *et al.* (1985) Betablockade during and after myocardial infarction: an overview of randomised trials. *Progressive Cardiovascular Disease* **27**: 335–71.

93   Flather M *et al.* (1997) Meta-analysis of individual patient data from trials of long term ACE inhibitor treatment after acute myocardial infarction (SAVE, AIRE, and Trace studies). *Circulation.* **96**(supplement): 1–706.

94   Hickie S, Ross S and Bond C (1998) A survey of the management of leg ulcers in primary care settings in Scotland. *Journal of Clinical Nursing.* **7**: 45–50.

95   Somerset M and Turton AP (1996) Impact of poor record keeping on leg ulcer care in general practice. *British Journal of Nursing.* **5**: 724, 726, 728 (passim).

96   NHS Executive (1999) *Patient and Public Involvement in the New NHS.* NHS Executive, London.

97   Dunning M, Abi-Aad G, Gilbert D *et al.* (1999) *Experience, Evidence and Everyday Practice.* King's Fund, London.

98   Coffey T, Boersma G, Smith L and Wallace P (eds) (1999) *Visions of Primary Care.* King's Fund, London.

99   Royal College of General Practitioners (1999) *Clinical Governance: practical advice for primary care in England and Wales.* Royal College of General Practitioners, London.

100   Poulton B and West M (1999) The determinants of effectiveness in primary health care teams. *Journal of Interprofessional Care.* **13**(1): 7–18.

101   Firth-Cozens J (1998) Elements that encourage good teamworking. *Quality in Health Care.* **7**(supplement).

102 Hart E and Fletcher J (1999) Learning how to change: a selective analysis of literature and experience of how teams learn and organisations change. *Journal of Interprofessional Care.* **13**(1): 53–63.

103 Chambers R and Davies M (1999) *What Stress in Primary Care!* Royal College of General Practitioners, London.

104 West M and Wallace M (1991) Innovation in health care teams. *European Journal of Social Psychology.* **21**: 303–15.

105 NHS Alliance (2000) *Implementing the Vision.* NHS Alliance, Retford.

106 Irvine D and Irvine S (eds) (1991) *Making Sense of Audit.* Radcliffe Medical Press, Oxford.

107 Donabedian A (1966) Evaluating the quality of medical care. *Millbank Memorial Fund Quarterly.* **44**: 166–204.

108 NHS Executive (1996) *Clinical Audit in the NHS. Using clinical audit in the NHS: a position statement.* NHS Executive, Leeds.

109 Maxwell R (1984) Quality assessment in health. *BMJ.* **288**: 1470–2.

110 Firth-Cozens J (1993) *Audit in Mental Health Services.* LEA, Hove.

111 Vuori H (1989) Research needs in quality assurance. *Quality Assurance in Health Care.* **1**(2/3): 147–59.

112 Walshe K and Coles J (1993) *Evaluating Audit. Developing a framework.* CASPE Research, London.

113 Chambers R and Milsom G (1995) *Audit of Contraceptive Services in Mid and North Staffordshire in Secondary Care, Primary Care and the Community.* University of Keele, Keele.

114 Jacobs B (1999) *A Theory of Change (ToC) Evaluation. A Health Action Zone Framework.* Centre for Health Policy and Practice, Staffordshire University, Stoke-on-Trent.

115 National Consumer Council (1995) *In Partnership with Patients.* National Consumer Council, London.

116 Crowley P (1998) *Involving the community in Primary Care Groups.* Abstract of presentation given at NHS Alliance national conference, Blackpool. Contact address: West End Health Resource Centre, Adelaide Terrace, Newcastle on Tyne NE4 8BE.

117 NHS Executive (1997) *Priorities and Planning Guidelines for the NHS: medium term priorities.* HMSO, London.

118 Regan E, Smith J and Shapiro J (1999) *First Off the Starting Blocks.* Health Services Management Centre, University of Birmingham, Birmingham.

119 Department of Health (1997) *Report on the Review of Patient-identifiable Information* (The Caldicott Committee report). Department of Health, London.

120 Pucci E, Belardinelli N and Signorino M (1999) Patients' understanding of randomised controlled trials depends on their education. *BMJ.* **318**: 875 (letter).

121 Healthy Sheffield Partnership (1996) *What You Said.* Healthy Sheffield Support Team, Town Hall Chambers, 1 Barker's Pool, Sheffield S1 1EN.

122 Murray SA, Tapson J, Turnbull L *et al.* (1994) Listening to local voices: adapting rapid appraisal to assess health and social needs in general practice. *BMJ.* **308**: 698–700.

123   McIver S (1998) *Healthy Debate? An independent evaluation of citizens' juries in health settings.* King's Fund, London.

124   Coote A (1999) Citizens' jury: a forum for health debate. *Update.* **18 March**: 485 (editorial).

125   Naidoo J and Wills J (1994) *Health Promotion: foundations for practice.* Ballière Tindall, London.

126   Beattie A (1991) In: Gabe J, Calnan M, Bury M. *The Sociology of the Health Service.* Routledge, London.

127   Tones K, Tilford S and Robinson Y (1990) *Health Education: effectiveness and efficiency.* Chapman & Hall, London.

128   Doxiadis S (ed) (1990) *Ethics in Health Promotion.* Wiley, Chichester.

129   Harris C and Dajda R (1996) The scale of repeat prescribing. *Br J Gen Pract.* **46**: 649–53.

130   National Audit Office (1993) *Repeat Prescribing by General Medical Practitioners in England.* HMSO, London.

131   NHS Executive (1997) *Prescription Fraud. An Efficiency Scrutiny.* Department of Health, London.

132   Medical Defence Union (1996) *Risk Management. Problems in general practice. Medication errors.* Medical Defence Union, London.

133   British Thoracic Society *et al.* (1997) The British guidelines on asthma management: 1995 review and position statement. *Thorax.* **52** (suppl 1): S1–21.

134   Higson N (1996) *Risk Management: health and safety in primary care.* Butterworth Heinemann, Oxford.

135   Chambers R, George V, McNeill A and Campbell I (1998) Health at work in the general practice. *Br J Gen Pract.* **48**: 1501–4.

136   Pligt J (1998) Perceived risk and vulnerability as predictors of precautionary behaviour. *Br J Health Psychology.* **3**: 1–14.

137   Carter Y and Thomas C (1997) *Research Methods in Primary Care.* Radcliffe Medical Press, Oxford.

138   Vallance P (1999) Cardiovascular risk assessment made easy. *Pulse.* **16 October**: 68.

139   *CardioRisk Manager.* BMJ Books, BMA House, London WC1H 9JR.

140   Grant J, Chambers E and Jackson G (1999) *The Good CPD Guide.* Reed Healthcare, Sutton.

141   Department of Health (1999) *Supporting Doctors, Protecting Patients.* Department of Health, London.

142   Scrivens E (1997) The impact of accreditation systems upon patient care. *Journal of Clinical Effectiveness.* **2**(4).

143   Scrivens E (1998) Policy issues in accreditation. *International Journal for Quality in Health Care.* **10**(1): 1–5.

144   Walshe K, Walsh N, Schofield T and Blakeway-Phillips C (eds) (2000) *Accreditation in Primary Care: towards clinical governance.* Radcliffe Medical Press, Oxford.

145   NHS Executive (1999) *The NHS Performance Assessment Framework.* DoH, London.

146   Donaldson L (1994) Doctors with problems in an NHS workforce. *BMJ.* **308**: 1277–82.

147   GPs Performance Project Steering Group (1997) *Screening and Educational Assessment.* South Thames Deanery.

148   North Staffordshire Health Authority (1998) *GPs Whose Performance Gives Cause for Concern.* North Staffordshire Health Authority, Stoke-on-Trent.

149   Birch K, Scrivens E and Field S (2000) *Quality in General Practice.* Radcliffe Medical Press, Oxford.

150   Baker S (1996) Use of performance indicators for general practice. *BMJ.* **312**: 58 (letter).

151   McColl A, Roderick P, Gabbay J (1998) Performance indicators for primary care groups: an evidence based approach. *BMJ.* **317**: 1354–60.

152   British Medical Association (1995) *Core Values for the Medical Profession in the 21st Century.* British Medical Association, London.

153   Royal College of General Practitioners and General Practitioners Committee (2000) *Good Medical Practice for General Practitioners.* Royal College of General Practitioners and General Practitioners Committee, London (consultation document).

154   Southgate L (1994) Freedom and discipline: clinical practice and the assessment of clinical competence. *Br J Gen Pract.* **44**: 87–92.

155   Irvine D (1997) The performance of doctors. 1: Professionalism and self regulation in a changing world. *BMJ.* **314**: 1540–2.

156   NHS Executive (1999) *Quality and Performance in the NHS: clinical indicators.* NHS Executive, Leeds.

157   Roland M (1999) Quality and efficiency: enemies or partners? *Br J Gen Pract.* **49**: 140–3.

158   General Practitioners Committee (1999) *Revalidation for clinical general practice.* Draft document for consultation. British Medical Association, London.

159   Rajaratnam G (1999) *Prioritising Health and Health Care in North Staffordshire: a proposal to establish a North Staffordshire Priorities Forum.* North Staffordshire Health Authority, Stoke-on-Trent.

160   Audit Commission (1999) *Protecting the Public Purse: ensuring probity in the NHS.* Audit Commission, London.

161   Accounts Commission for Scotland (1998) *Annual Report.* Accounts Commission for Scotland, Edinburgh.

162   NHS Executive (1998) *Countering Fraud in the NHS.* NHS Executive, London.

163   Department of Health (1999) *The NHS Performance Assessment Framework.* Health Service Circular HSC 1999/078. Department of Health, London.

164   Francis B and Humphreys J (1999) Enrolled nurses and the professionalism of nursing: a comparison of nurse education and skill-mix in Australia and the UK. *International Journal of Nursing Studies.* **36**: 127–35.

165   Sakr M *et al.* (1999) Care of minor injuries by emergency nurse practitioners or junior doctors: a randomised controlled trial. *Lancet.* **354**: 1321–6.

166 Marsh GN and Dawes ML (1995) Establishing a minor illness nurse in a busy general practice. *BMJ.* **310**: 778–80.

167 Jenkins-Clarke S, Care-Hill R and Dixon P (1998) Teams and seams: skill mix in primary care. *Journal of Advanced Nursing.* **28**: 1120–6.

168 Vorster M (1999) Practice management. Behind the lines. *Health Service Journal.* **109**: 24–5.

169 Fall M *et al.* (1997) An evaluation of a nurse-led ear care service in primary care: benefits and costs. *Br J Gen Pract.* **47**: 699–703.

170 Calpin-Davies PJ and Akehurst RL (1999) Doctor–nurse substitution: the workforce equation. *Journal of Nurse Management.* **7**: 71–9.

171 Smith DC and Davies L (1997) Who contributes to the public health function? *Journal of Public Health.* **19**: 451–6.

172 Wells WD (1998) Having a practice pharmacist can reduce prescribing costs. *BMJ.* **317**: 473.

173 Gill P (1996) The importance of workforce planning in the NHS in the 1990s. *Health Manpower Management.* **22**: 21–5.

174 Department of Health (1998) *Management of Health Safety and Welfare Issues for NHS Staff.* Health Service Circular HSC 1998/064. Department of Health, London.

175 Sen D and Osborne K (1997) General practices and health and safety at work. *Br J Gen Pract.* **47**: 103–4.

176 White RR and Smith JM (1995) Infection control in general practice: results of a questionnaire survey. *Journal of Public Health.* **17**: 146–9.

177 Chambers R (1999) *Survival Skills for GPs.* Radcliffe Medical Press, Oxford.

178 Cabello CC (1999) Six stepping stones to better management. *Nurse Manager.* **30**: 39–40.

179 Drummond MF, O'Brien B, Stoddart GL and Torrance GW (1997) *Methods for the Economic Evaluation of Health Care Programmes* (2e). Oxford University Press, Oxford.

180 Cuschieri A (1995) Whither minimal access surgery: tribulations and expectations. *American Journal of Surgery.* **169**: 9–19.

181 NHS Centre for Reviews and Disease (1999) Getting evidence into practice. *Effective Health Care.* **5**: 1–16.

182 Donnan S (1998) The health of adult Europe: combating inequalities involves measuring what counts. *BMJ.* **316**: 1620–1.

183 Cleary PD (1997) Subjective and objective measures of health: which is better when? *J Health Serv Res Policy.* **2**: 3–4.